The Ultimate Book Club Experience
HOW TO CREATE & MAINTAIN A SUCCESSFUL BOOK CLUB

The Ultimate Book Club Experience
HOW TO CREATE & MAINTAIN A SUCCESSFUL BOOK CLUB

TaNisha Webb

The Ultimate Book Club Experience: How to Create and
Maintain a Successful Book Club
Copyright © 2012 TaNisha Webb
Book Club 101 Publications

ISBN-13: 978-0615644677
ISBN-10: 0615644678

Library of Congress Control Number: 2012909872

First Printing June 2012
Printed in United States of America

DEDICATION

This book is dedicated to my aunt Zanetta Montgomery who I know continues to cheer me on from Heaven as she always did on Earth.

I love you dearly. I think about you daily. I miss you terribly.

I hope I continue to make you proud.

TABLE OF CONTENTS

ACKNOWLEDGEMENTS

I have so many people to thank throughout the years so please be patient with me. It's not often that someone can say that they published their first book. ☺ And ya'll know I love to talk so there's my disclaimer! lol

First I want to thank God for giving me the ability to understand that my passion is a gift and that I shouldn't waste it. Some people never realize their passion or just don't act on them. Otherwise, this book wouldn't have ever come to light, let alone anything that I've done thus far.

I want to thank my parents Sherry Simon and Charles Simon. Thanks mom for always helping out and also for being a great woman to look up to throughout the years. I'm who I am today because of how you raised me. I appreciate everything that you've gone through to raise me properly. Daddy - you were the first person that made want to read because of your love for books. You've taught me that reading books and listening to music is just as entertaining as sitting in front of a television set growing up. Your passion for making music encouraged me to embrace my calling, even if no one else understood it. I've learned to create my own lane and that it's better to stand out and be noticed, instead of blending in. Your love for music has served as a model for my literary journey.

To my baby girl Shayla Williams – I can say that I'm truly blessed to have you as a daughter. You are the most kind- hearted and generous person that I know. You have been my motivation to always do better from the moment that you were conceived. I owe my success to you. I hope this book serves as a reminder that you can do anything that you choose to do in life. Do what you feel that's right in your heart and you'll never go wrong. Thank you for making me a proud parent.

To my siblings: Domitric (Lady), Ebony, LeVar, Denise (Niecy) and Mary (Polly). Thank you for all of the love, support and encouragement throughout the years. I love you all dearly.

Thanks to all of my extended family as well. You all are wonderful and I love you all.

Shantèe Jacques, Sharetta Simmons, Traci Baker, Chree Payne and Keisha Brooks - You ladies have gone above and beyond in supporting me since way back when. You all hold a special place in my heart for different reasons and I thank you for being true friends in every sense of the word. I love you all.

Michael Gipson – You were the first person to tell me that I should write a book. This book isn't quite what you had in mind but ummm...it's a book no less! lol ☺ Much love to you, my friend.

Jeff Strong - Thanks so much for being so adamant about me writing this book. You were my constant reminder that I had work to do and refused to let me rest until my book was complete. You are always the one person to always ask, "How can I help you reach your goals?" You'll never know how much that has meant to me over the years. Your business knowledge has been so valuable to me. I appreciate all the time that you've invested in me. Lots of love to you.

Curtis Bunn – I could try to thank you a million times and I don't think it would honestly hit the surface of how incredibly appreciative I am to you and the National Book Club Conference. Attending NBCC has completely changed my life and I will always be grateful to you. Thanks a million! ☺

Martin Pratt – Good, bad or indifferent; thanks so much for all that you've done for me. Your insight has been Heaven sent. I appreciate you!

Jonathan Hearn - Thanks for always being in my corner. Your support means a lot.

To the wonderful ladies of the KC Girlfriends Book Club, past and present - I can't imagine what my life would have been like had I not moved to Kansas City in 2003. You ladies are a blessing and I thank you from the bottom of my heart for your friendship and support. Our book club experiences has not only been the blueprint for this book but has already helped other book clubs get their start. We have truly grown as a family and I love you all.

Mrs. Paris Lipsey-Coley – You are the most real person on the planet! Thank you so much for my first book club experience during the Book Expression Book Club days. It was the best co-ed book club experience ever. I'm still amazed how we never got thrown out of Barnes and Nobles due to our lively conversations discussing books written by Eric Jerome Dickey and E. Lynn Harris! lol You have been such a blessing to Shayla and I. Words cannot express how thankful I am to have you in our lives.

Sisters Sippin' Tea Literary Group Tulsa Chapter aka the lil' Book Club That Could ☺ - You ladies seriously rock! When I grow up I want to be just like you. ☺ Thanks so much for being such a prime example of what a book club can do with a lot of determination, great vision and hard work. I want to thank you ladies from the bottom of my heart for all of the support that you've given me over the years. I want to personally thank Sharon Haynes for always checking up on me. You are a blessing.

Oh, Ms. Ebony Farashuu! Where do I begin? I believe that people come into your life for a reason. I knew you were special from the first moment that you reached out to my book club prior to releasing *Slow Burn*. Thanks for taking the time to edit my book and valuable feedback. I couldn't have chosen a better person to be a part of this project. It's only a matter of time when the rest of the world discovers just how truly talented you are. You're one of the best authors on the planet!

Sonya Ward – Everyone need someone like you in their life! Thanks so much for all of the late night talks about EVERYTHING. You have been so kind to me, full of ideas, and encouragement. Thank you from the bottom of my heart for everything that you've done for me. You're a gem.

To my book club president sisters: Lisa R. Johnson, Tasha Martin, Margaret Bullocks, Tiffany Bridges, Tee C. Royal, Toni Robinson, Sheyvette Dinkens – You're all amazing and I'm so proud to be in the company of other great book clubs.

To THE Black Book Club Experience Social Network and all of the book club presidents that encouraged me to write this book – I hope I've made you proud.

Michelle Buckley - You recognized everything that I was capable of accomplishing before I ever did. Watching you during your journey has taught me that an author's work is never done, regardless if they are traditional or self published. Watching your literary journey has made me learn to appreciate talented and underexposed authors like yourself, which is what made the KC Girlfriends Book Club adopt the idea of reading new and underexposed authors. You are an amazing sister and I thank you for allowing me to get to know you.

Michelle T. Johnson - Thank you so much for giving me pointers on how to write a reference book. You have been a great example of how someone can take their passion and actually get PAID! I so want to be like you when I grow up! ☺

A'ndrea Wilson - Your insight has been so helpful. Thanks so much for always giving me honest feedback regardless if I asked for it or not! lol Everyone needs that one person that can give them the truth, along with the knowledge to back up what they are saying. Thanks for being such a wonderful soundboard!

Trice Hickman and T.L. James - You both rock! Thanks so much for always believing in me and for sitting down and giving me a crash course in self publishing!

Brian W. Smith - Thanks so much for your valuable insight and for being a great example of how to conduct business.

Tiffany L. Warren - Thanks so much for all of your help and support throughout the years with literary event planning and helping me to understand the publishing industry.

Dee Stewart, Dana Pittman and Sylvia Hubbard - Thanks so much for your marketing sense and for sharing your knowledge with me.

Ella Curry - You are one of the most generous people I know. Thank you for always being so supportive and willing to give me valuable information.

Jo Lena Johnson - Thanks so much for your expertise. You are awesome.

I also want to thank all of the great authors that has propelled readers to create book clubs in the first place. It's because of your passion for writing that make us come together in the first place. I think I can speak for all book clubs when I say that we love you and encourage you all to continue giving us something to talk about. You're not only gaining fans but helping to create book club but extended families.

If I've forgotten anyone that has been a blessing to me throughout my life and literary journey please do not take it personal. You are truly appreciated and I thank you as well.

TaNisha Webb

INTRODUCTION

Creating a book club can be a hard but rewarding journey. One of the most challenging parts of creating a book club is not having any idea where to start. This book was created to give you practical steps in order to create the right book club for you. You will find that each chapter is designed to walk you through the process of creating a solid foundation for your book club from the beginning to the end. At the end of most of the chapters you will find an exercise, which are designed to help you make critical decisions regarding your book club.

I think one of the most challenging parts of having an established book club is maintaining it. Knowing how to keep your book club in great shape can feel like a job most times. Coming up with great ideas to keep the book club enjoyable or just simply in existence can be a task, especially if you've haven't established relationships with other book club presidents. I've learned that no one will understand what you're going through quite like another book club president will. This is how I've been able to stay sane and keep moving forward. ☺

This book was created following a mere suggestion by some of the sister book clubs that I've had the pleasure of mentoring and befriending throughout the years. You will learn that your sister book clubs can be an enormous benefit towards the success of your book club because of the support that they offer. This wonderful resource guide will also benefit you as well by offering a reference point to help you make the best decisions for your book club by offering you a step by step guide, along with critical thinking exercise to help you create a strategic plan in order to create a solid foundation for your book club.

I hope this book club resource guide will help take some of the "guess work" out of creating and maintaining a successful book club for you. Please be sure to visit my website to contact me and for other book club resources. www.tanishawebbonline.com.

Stay Blessed & Well Read,

TaNisha Webb

TANISHA'S BOOK CLUB JOURNEY

How It All Began

My book club experience began in 1999, in my hometown Wichita, KS. My good friend Paris and I would discuss a variety of books that we had read with one another. Paris had other friends that read as well and soon decided that we should create a book club, particularly because she was tired of discussing the book over and over again with several of her friends at separate times. Our group was a co-ed book club, which really made our book club experience fun and edgy. We met in a local Barnes and Nobles, where they spoiled us with a thirty percent discount on our book purchases, complimentary freshly baked cookies, and a space to discuss our monthly selections. Or group was easily excitable, especially when we were discussing great topics. Barnes and Noble probably weren't ready for us, nor were their patrons. We would find ourselves in great debates over E. Lynn Harris and Eric Jerome Dickey novels and it wasn't uncommon for us to have patrons weigh in on our discussions. By the time we left we were almost certain that Barnes and Noble would never allow us back in their doors, but that never happened.

It was a great experience that I shared with my friends, which felt like family. We kept the book club together for about a year, but our individual priorities began to change. Most of my friends were single mothers attending college, some were married and taking care of children, and we also had a few members that didn't have any children but were dealing with life issues. By the time the book club ended, we were more a social club than a book club. No one was reading the entire book and we were not ready to discuss anything. We tried to revitalize the book club in 2003, but around that time I had been offered a job in Kansas City. I left Wichita and began my journey with new my career in hand.

Kansas City Here I Come!

My daughter and I moved to the Kansas City Metro area in June of 2003. I was busy getting into my new career after receiving my degree in Respiratory Therapy and only knew one person that lived in the area. I decided that I wanted to meet women in the area outside of my job and began looking for a book club to join. I browsed some popular literary resource websites but found their book club lists to be sorely outdated. When using the email addresses provided by the sites, I received many undeliverable emails, or received no response at all. I then came across a local African American social event website where a young lady was recruiting new members for her group called, 'Girlfriends Book Club.' The book club met at Tea Drops, a small but eclectic tea shop in a popular area of town. The ladies were very nice and welcoming and I felt a good vibe from them. We met a few times but, as with my previous group, the members began to drop out due to various obligations. The book club decreased to two members, I, and a woman named Tiffany. We continued to meet each month at Tea Drops, but eventually stopped reading books and just met up to go out to eat. In 2004, we decided to begin soliciting members again online and slowly added members.

At this time, I viewed myself only as the representative for the book club and definitely not the book club president. I had no desire to become a book club president and planned on turning over the reins to someone else. I just wanted to be present at meetings and go on about my life until we met again. As time went by, that didn't happen and I accepted the presidency role for the reading group now known as the KC Girlfriends Book Club.

Our book club's name was inevitably changed by local author Michelle Buckley, whom I befriended during the release of her first book, Bulletproof Soul. Michelle was looking for local book clubs that she could sit down with and discuss her book. At the time, I was green about hosting authors and wondered why any author would want to discuss their book with us. What if we didn't like the book? What were we supposed to say to them? We only had four members at this time. As I spoke with Michelle about sitting down with my book club, she and I decided that maybe we should invite other book clubs to discuss her book together. Michelle took it beyond a mere book discussion and ended up coordinating a huge book release party that was unlike anything I had experienced. Michelle created an award named after her book, Bulletproof Soul, which she presented to different women that had faced adversity within the community. She asked various local book club presidents to present these women with Bulletproof Soul awards. I was one of the few that she chose to be a presenter. This was the first time that I had ever presented in front of a group of people and I was terrified. It was around this time that Michelle felt that the book club's name should be changed to the KC Girlfriends Book Club because it not only kept with the girlfriends theme but also helped to define where we were located so it would set us apart from other book clubs that may decide to use the same name. After many times of correcting Michelle, we decided that we actually liked the name and kept it. Befriending Michelle is actually what made our group want to support new and underexposed authors. To this day my book club still reads ninety percent new authors.

Within a year and a half of us revitalizing our group, we grew from two to forty-one members. It was incredible. There wasn't a lot to our book club. We met once a month in a selected restaurant and discussed our book. That's it, that's all. About half of the members would show up at a time, which was fine with me because trying to facilitate a large group in a public place had its challenges. Dues and bylaws were incorporated into our book club in 2005, which helped to cut our membership in half. Although dues were only $24 per year, most didn't see the point in paying dues if they weren't regularly attending the meetings, which was exactly the result that I wanted.

The National Book Club Conference

Our book club's mission and foundation was actually better defined in 2006, after my book club decided to attend the National Book Club Conference (NBCC) in Atlanta, GA. About six members attended this year where we expected to just have the opportunity to meet up with our favorite authors during a fun-filled weekend. Well that did happen, but what we weren't expecting was to come back a better book club because we had experienced NBCC. NBCC is truly a standalone literary conference that caters to book clubs from all over the country. It is like an annual literary family reunion with your favorite authors and book clubs. Not only did we sit in many different book club meetings with authors, we were able to listen to various panel discussions. One of my favorite panel discussions is called, "Maximizing Your Book Club Experience," which is staffed by different book clubs. This is the one time during the conference where we are able to learn about what other book clubs were doing in order to keep their groups viable. This panel discussion is what changed the direction of the KC Girlfriends Book Club and I will always be grateful to the staff of NBCC, Curtis Bunn, all of authors and book clubs that we were able to meet and get to know since attending in 2006. After leaving NBCC we were so inspired by listening to other book clubs that we began making changes to improve our book club experience immediately.

The KC Girlfriends Book Club Radio Show

In February 2008, I decided to expand the book club and create a radio show. Truth be told, the radio show was not something that I wanted to do in the beginning. It was a suggestion by author Michelle Buckley, which I basically decided to politely ignore in the beginning. One thing I've learned about hanging out with Michelle is that she's full of ideas all the time, which will keep me busy - all the time! I began listening to radio shows on Blog Talk Radio in 2007. During this time, there was one book club with a radio show but they had only broadcasted two shows and that was it. I began listening to more literary radio shows and basically tried to figure out what my radio show's niche would be. Initially the premise for the radio show was to help my book club members connect with some of the authors that we had chosen to read. Most new and underexposed authors simply do not have the funds to travel across the country to meet with every book club that decides to read their book. Since there wasn't any other book clubs hosting a radio show at the time, I felt that the show should represent exactly what our book club already believed in; create a foundation so that new and underexposed authors could have the well deserved exposure to a broader audience. It was also important that I created a platform to help support my sister book clubs and literary resources. We've had many panel discussions and authors come on the show to help educate and open up a dialog on a variety of topics. In 2008 and 2010, the KC Girlfriends Book Club was recognized with a Community Service award for our dedication to supporting authors and our literary community by the National Book Club Conference.

From Radio Show Host to Panel Discussion Moderator and Creating Social Networks & Coordinating Literary Events

For me, my book club journey has taken me through some surprising twists and turns and has given me some recognition in the literary community. This wasn't at all what I was seeking in the very beginning but it has been beneficial as I've moved forward with the many projects that we embarked on. Along with being a book club president and the host and creator of the KC Girlfriends Book Club Radio Show, I began moderating the "Maximizing Your Book Club Experience" panel discussion at NBCC in 2008.

In 2009, I helped create a social network called THE Black Book Club Experience, which is a support system for book club presidents from all over the country, which provides supports from fellow book club presidents with keeping their book club going. I also started a line of bookmarks called, Bookmark It! Handcrafted Bookmarks, which started out as a project to create a keepsake for guests during my book club's literary retreat.

Due to so many inquiries regarding how to create and maintain a book club, I decided to create, The Ultimate Book Club Experience, a resource website exclusively for book clubs and individuals that wanted more information on creating and maintaining book clubs. In 2010, I founded and coordinated my first literary event in Kansas City called, Fall Into Books Literary Conference, which hosted 30 authors, including Eric Jerome Dickey, ReShonda Tate Billingsley, Victoria Christopher Murray, J.D. Mason and many more great authors.

In 2011, I decided to take The Ultimate Book Club Experience website one step further and wanted to provide a more structured approach for anyone interested in creating and maintaining a book club. I created Book Club 101 University, which is a website that offers weekly blogs, quarterly ecourses on various book club topics, and also resources. In May 2011, I held the first online book club conference called Book Club University Online Conference, a five hour webinar that addressed various book club topics and was presented by some of the best book club presidents around the country, along with interviews with some of our favorite authors.

Book Club 101 Magazine

Book Club 101 Magazine is the first of its kind. The magazine was designed solely to keep book clubs connected by creating articles specifically for book clubs, while still connecting readers to authors and literary events. The magazine also provides helpful tips, book reviews, contests, book discussion sessions, recipes and more.

The idea for the magazine came to me in 2011 while I was helping one of my colleagues with ideas for his literary magazine. We began to discuss how many literary websites and magazines are made for authors and other literary entities as far as content was concerned. The only articles that were generally geared towards readers and book clubs were the occasional book club spotlights, interviews of some of our favorite authors and book reviews. At this point I became frustrated with what I felt was a lack of support to help inform and educate book clubs. It was with that same energy that I began planning the launch of the magazine. The idea of launching a magazine is very scary but exciting. Because this type of magazine has never been done before; I didn't know if my idea would actually pay off. I had no idea how to put a magazine together but I've always had a great eye for details and knew what a magazine should look like to make it attractive and engaging. So I did months of research to see how I could make it happen. I literally built the magazine from scratch with free magazine design software and templates. With the encouragement and support from my literary family and a lot of hard work and sleepless nights, the magazine took shape and launched on February 25, 2012.

I can honestly say that my book club experience has taken me on a very interesting and unexpected journey. My passion for reading has truly been a blessing and has allowed me to really step into my own. I think everyone has a passion for something. I did everything in my power to ignore my passion and move on with my career as a respiratory therapist, but God truly has another plan for me. My literary journey has been very unconventional, unpredictable and weird all rolled up in one! Becoming a literary trailblazer is an amazing feeling. So I say to you, if you have a passion to start a book club, it will happen. Take your time, be patient, and flexible in order to create the right book club for you. Hopefully this book will take a lot of the guess work out of creating and maintaining a book club and help you along your journey.

CHAPTER 1

THE FOUNDATION OF A BOOK CLUB

Overview

Forming a book club is like building a house. Without the proper materials, the foundation of your book club will be weak. Before creating a book club, it is important to understand the purpose of a reading group and why the book club experience is such a wonderful thing!

Objectives

- Learn the definition of a book club

- Learn about what the book club experience is about

- Identify reasons to create a book club

- Identify principles for your book club

- Establish goals for your book club

- Decide which services to provide for your book club

The Purpose of a Book Club

The main purpose for creating a book club is to commune with a group of people that love to read and discuss books. However, many of today's book clubs are doing more than just meeting once per month to discuss books. Book clubs are now becoming non-profit organizations. They also coordinate fabulous events and offer community based services, and more.

Book clubs are, essentially, the heartbeat of the literary industry. Without book clubs, many authors would not be as successful. Book clubs are a free marketing tool for authors because they are always eager to talk about great a book, which in turn helps to spread the author's work by word of mouth. Book clubs also have a tendency to support authors throughout their careers by buying their books. An author that creates a relationship with a book club is more likely to have fans for the lifetime of their writing career.

Beyond the obvious reasons for creating a book club, you may have other specific goals that differ from others. However, all literacy groups have a common thread; they love to read and discuss books, while supporting their favorite authors.

The Book Club Experience

The book club experience is quite unique. People who are not avid readers or have never been involved in a book club may find it hard to understand why anyone would want to sit around and discuss books with a group of people every month. Book clubs are more than just about discussing books. Books clubs are the back bone for authors, especially African American authors. Word of mouth is a crucial marketing tool for authors. Book clubs love to talk about their favorite reads and are always willing to spread the word, which is music to an author's ears!

One of the great benefits of being in a book club is having the chance to sit with authors to discuss their work. I can personally tell you that there is nothing like it. Authors are wonderful guests at book club meetings because they tend to answer all of the questions members may not have a chance to ask during a public event.

Outside of book club meetings, book clubs have become more socially conscious. This has caused book clubs to become more involved in their communities by raising awareness for literacy and literature.

Book clubs come in all shapes, sizes, religions, genres and genders, which is what makes each book club unique. This is your chance to create a phenomenal literary group. Allow your love for literature to guide your way to a successful and healthy book club experience.

Many book club members become close, forming a literary extension of your family. By discussing books and what they mean to your lives, you will learn many things about one another. Through these experiences, your bond will strengthen. It's truly amazing how discussing books can bring a group of people closer. It is my hope that you are able to have a great book club experience as you create the perfect book club for you!

Identify Your Reasons for Creating a Book Club

It is important to identify your specific reasons for wanting to create a book club. There is no right or wrong answer unless you are using the organization for personal gain.

Examples of personal gain are as follows:

- Creating a book club in order to sell a specific author's work

- Creating a book club in order to gain clientele for a non-literary based business

These are generally not good reasons to create a book club and can often lead to an early demise for your group. Remembering why you created your book club is imperative. Recognizing and keeping your goal in mind will help keep your group on track, reminding everyone why you gravitated towards each other to begin with.

Identify Your Book Club's Principles and Purpose

Deciding what principles will support your book club's foundation is one of most important components in creating consistency within your group. Identifying those principles will help your book club set a standard and define your book club's purpose. This can also help with determining if you have the right members in your book club. Upholding the core principles of the book club will ensure that you and your members are on the same page, and that you are protecting the book club and what it stands for. Think about the vision you have for your book club and come up with the principles that you feel that your club should adhere to.

Establish Goals

Where would you like your book club to be in two months? Six months? Two years? Determine obtainable goals for your book club, but concentrate on getting your group established before you attempt to conquer them. It takes a strong group of individuals who are on the same page, get along, and see the value of carrying out these goals in order to accomplish them. Jotting down these milestones and discussing them with your book club members early on will give them an idea of where you're trying to take the book club in the future. It will also allow you to observe your potential members as you lay out your plans. This will allow you to get a sense of which members will be supportive of your ideas.

Once you've established your milestones, set a reasonable timeline for when you'd like to reach each one. Staying on track is important, but you must understand that you may have to adjust your timeline here and there, depending on the dynamic of your book club. Again, it's more important that you establish a solid book club before you begin to add more responsibilities so that neither you nor your members become overwhelmed.

Deciding Which Services to Provide

Providing different services is purely optional but it's a great way to connect with other literary-minded people and your community. One service that is widely appreciated by authors is providing feedback in the form of book reviews.

Providing community-based services like reading programs or coordinating book drives can set your book club a part while allowing your book club to give back to the community.

Book clubs that go beyond discussing books are a very important resource for their communities. Networking is essential to the success of any community project or event. Not only will you be rewarded personally with knowing that you helped others, but you are also establishing a support system, when and if you ever decide to create events or spearhead a community project.

Now that we've discussed the foundation and purpose of a book club and the book club experience, let's take a moment to see where you are with creating a book club. If you already have a book club established go through the exercise and see if your book club is where you'd like it to be.

CHAPTER 1 EXERCISE

THINKING IT THROUGH

In order for you to begin building the foundation for your book club, it's important that you know why you're creating a book club. More importantly you should be certain that you are starting a book club for the right reasons. You must remember your specific reasons for creating your book club to help you stay focused and keep your book club grounded. Get familiar with the answers that you provide in this exercise, as we will be using your answers to create your mission statement later on in the book.

Answer the following questions:

1. Name 5 reasons you would like to create a book club.

2. Name 4 principles that you would like your book club to follow.

3. Write down 3 goals or accomplishments you would like your book club to achieve.

4. Name 2 different services you would like your book club to provide.

CHAPTER 1 NOTES

CHAPTER 1 NOTES

CHAPTER TWO

ARE YOU READY TO CREATE A BOOK CLUB?

Overview

Most people who decide to create a book club do so because they absolutely love to read and wish to discuss great books with others. Often, people fail to realize that creating a book club takes much time and dedication. The foundation for your book club must be carefully laid out, or it will potentially fail within the first year. This chapter is designed to prepare you for the work ahead.

Objectives

- Discuss five elements for creating a successful book club

- Identify a book club president's responsibilities

- How to choose the right people to help support your new book club

Five Essential Elements to Creating a Successful Book Club

There are five essential elements that must be in place in order to create a successful book club. I always ask these questions when someone expresses an interest in beginning a book club. The five essential elements that must be present are as follow:

- You must be an avid reader.

- You must have good reading habits.

- You must be able to make time to meet on a consistent basis.

- You must have great organizational skills.

- You must be a people person and be able to deal with different personalities.

So now that we've identified the five essential elements to creating a book club, let's discuss each of these elements in detail.

You Must Be an Avid Reader

Serious book clubs are not meant to encourage casual readers to read more. Instead, book clubs are meant to help provide an outlet for avid readers to discuss books with other avid readers. In order to keep the interest within your book club going, you and your members must be able to keep up with the reading materials. You, as the president or founder, should be a primary example of this simple but important rule by reading the book of the month selections, even if you dislike the book! If your members see that you're not keeping up with the reading materials, this will ultimately give them permission to stop reading as well. This will hurt your book club over time. Remember, even horrible books can be discussed. It's more important that you're supporting the member that suggested the book instead of not completing the book. Over time, you will be able to tell which genres work best for your book club. Sometimes the issue is not the book but more so the genre not being the right fit for your book club. Book clubs should be open to reading new authors and genres. This will keep your book club fresh and exciting. So, until you begin to suspect that a specific genre is not for the book club, be sure to give it a fair chance first.

What's the difference between an avid reader and a casual reader? Avid readers love to read. An avid reader will make time to read on a regular basis because it's a part of their daily routine. Avid readers also tend to be bothered by editing issues in a book and often have problems getting past them no matter how fantastic the storyline may be.

Generally, casual readers are not as critical as avid readers are. The casual reader may not see editing issues as a big deal and feel that a great story line is worth overlooking the errors. Casual readers tend to have issues completing the selected book of the month in a timely fashion because they are leisure readers. Casual readers tend to pick up a book and read it over a longer period of time, where avid readers generally can't put a book down and will complete two or more books a month.

You may also find that casual readers are not always an effective or engaged member during book discussions. Remember, your group is only as strong as your members. If you allow members who habitually fail to complete the required reading to remain in your group, other members may follow suit. This can set a negative tone for your book club.

TaNisha's Pearl of Wisdom

Do not keep members in your group that will not keep up with reading the book selections. The point of being a part of a book club is to be able to thoroughly discuss the book with others. If you allow such members to continue to participate in your book club, your book club will eventually turn into a social club. You should remind your group from time to time about the importance of completing the books in time to discuss for the meetings. The only other option outside of not completing the book is to not come to the meeting. Remember: Book club first! Social club later!

You Must Have Good Reading Habits

Avid readers read as much as they can as a favorite pastime, even if their schedule is hectic. As a book club president, you should ensure that you have enough time in your schedule to read at least one novel per month. For an avid reader reading, one novel per month definitely indicates that they've had a busy month! Most avid readers are able to read at least two or more novels during a month's time. One key question that you should ask your incoming members is how many books they read per month for pleasure. This will give you a good idea how much leisure time they may have to read, which will help indentify if they are able to handle being in a book club.

You Must Be Able to Meet on a Consistent Basis

Once your book club is underway, it is important that you are able to set aside a specific day and time for your meetings in order to be consistent. This will help build up anticipation each month to discuss that great book! It will also help your members plan around the meetings. If you or your members move book club meetings around, it will make it hard for everyone to keep up with what's going on, and may eventually discourage them from participating. It's important that you give the same amount of time in between meetings for your members to purchase and read the next month's book. Creating a successful book club takes someone that is able to offer consistency. Everyone should know that every third Saturday at 5 pm the book club will meet. This will allow everyone to clear their schedules and regularly attend meetings.

You Must Have Great Organizational Skills

Creating a book club takes great organization skills. Even if you decide to delegate responsibilities to other members, it's still your job to keep up with everything that's going on with YOUR book club. You are the one that will initially set up the structure of your book club, which will help to create a template in order to keep your book club on the right track. It will also make it easy for someone to assist you with duties that you may want to delegate out.

It's very important that if you decide to delegate responsibilities to others that you choose people that understand and support the mission and goals of the book club. This person(s) should also be an effective member of your book club, regularly attend meetings, and able to participate in discussions.

TaNisha's Pearl of Wisdom

Okay this is real talk! If you have to track down a member to get the information that you need, your book club will fall apart. Do not allow members that do not display good organizational skills or that cannot be found when you need information regarding the book club to hold a major position. Do what's best for your book club and only delegate duties out to people that display loyalty to the book club, support the book club's mission, and that you can truly trust and count on. Always know what's going on with the book club by asking for regular updates. In other words: **KEEP UP WITH WHAT'S GOING ON WITH YOUR BOOK CLUB AT ALL TIMES!**

You Must Be a People Person and Be Able to Deal with Different Personalities

It's really important that your people skills are on point. If you're not a people person and have a problem with dealing with different personalities, you should just stop now and not waste your time trying to create a book club. Book clubs are fun because the members all share the love for reading. Outside of the fact that books essential core for the group, your book club members may be like night and day! Your book club will be more interesting if your members are not necessarily in the same age group or gender. It's the life experiences, age, gender and different thought process that will make your book club rich and very interesting. Book clubs that stay in a certain age range tend to fall flat because the member's life experiences are mostly the same or their mindset is very similar. Good conversations begin with different life experiences. Books are what bring people together but it's each member's life experiences that gives the book club richness and allows the group to bond.

Now that we're clear on the five essentials to creating a successful book club, let's talk a little bit about book club responsibilities and finding support to pull your book club together!

Book Club President Responsibilities

As a book club president, you can expect to have many responsibilities in order to insure that your book club is running smoothly. Even if you decide to delegate duties, you will ultimately have others look to you to maintain order and solve issues within the book group. Creating a book club takes a lot of dedication and hard work! Did you read the hard work part!?

I can personally tell you that being a book club president is very rewarding but there is a great amount of work and responsibility that is required in order for my book club to be successful. Having great book club members will help you keep your book club moving forward in the right direction. You will basically be the anchor for all of your members, which is a great thing but with this new responsibility, you will inevitably be the counselor, go to person, shoulder to cry on, peacemaker and more. Your book club will eventually become an extension of your family so expect to have a family-like atmosphere once everyone becomes comfortable around one another. Remember that your book club is only as strong as its members but at the same time you set the tone for your book club. If you're consistent, your book club members will also be consistent.

TaNisha's Pearl of Wisdom

If you're not consistent and organized, your book club will be a hot mess! Plain, simple, and straight to the point!

Finding Support for Your Book Club

Now that you've decided to create a book club, it's very important that you find the right support for your new book club. Create a list of friends, family members and coworkers that you know are avid readers and that you feel will have enough time to read and discuss books on a consistent basis. Once you have your list together go back over the list and weed out all of the people that you KNOW have the potential to cause drama. Now, look at your list and choose a few people that you can trust and run your idea to start a book club by them. They will more than likely give you some great ideas and also be willing to help you create your book club. Note: Some people work better with a few people to create a book club and some may decide to create a book club without any help. Figure out which one you are before you decide to allow people to help you create your book club. Whichever way you decide to go is entirely up to you, but I can tell you that it's much easier to have the help and support of one or two people instead of going it alone. We'll talk more about recruiting members outside of creating your support system in a later chapter.

One other thing that you may want to do while you're trying to create your book club is to reach out to a local book club, if you can find one. If you cannot find a local book club find one online. Book club presidents are usually very friendly and are willing to answer questions and help provide valuable resources for you as you go through the process of creating your book club.

CHAPTER 2 EXERCISE

DO YOU HAVE TIME TO CREATE A BOOK CLUB?

Now that you have a better idea of what to expect as a book club president and what you need to have in place in order to begin a successful book club, let's see where you are in creating your book club!

Answer yes or no to the following questions.
Total your yes answers <u>only</u>.

1. Are you an avid reader?
   Yes ☐ No ☐

2. Do you have enough time in your schedule to consistently read at least one novel each month?
   Yes ☐ No ☐

3. Do you have a consistent day and time within your schedule to set aside for book club meetings?
   Yes ☐ No ☐

4. Do you have good organizational skills?
   Yes ☐ No ☐

5. Are you a people person and able to deal with different personalities?
   Yes ☐ No ☐

Total Yes Answers ☐

Let's Discuss Your Results

5 yes responses
You are now one step closer to making your book club a reality! You should definitely move forward with creating your book club!

3-4 yes responses
You should work on these important keys that you answered no to before moving on with your book club vision. Some of the things that may need to be adjusted may not take long to work through. But I'm confident that it won't be long before you can move forward to creating your book club!

0-2 yes responses
You should definitely not move forward at this time to create your book club, but instead work on these important keys when time permits and then go for it! This will also give you even more time to jot down ideas for your book club so when you're actually ready to create your book club, you'll have a clear book club vision!

CHAPTER 2 NOTES

CHAPTER 2 NOTES

CHAPTER 3

STEPS TO CREATING A SUCCESSFUL BOOK CLUB

Overview

Okay so now that you're clear on how to build a solid foundation and know the essential elements of creating a successful book club, it's important that you think about what type of book club you'd like to create. There are many different components that you'll need to think about before you recruit your members. Chapter three will walk you through the different types of book clubs and help you to really make crucial decisions so that your book club has a great start!

Objectives

- Learn the pros and cons of location base and online book club

- Learn how to create a membership criteria

- Key questions to ask potential members

- Discuss how to create a membership application

- Discuss how to recruit members

- How to prepare for a meet & greet and first book club meeting

Online vs. Location Based Book Clubs

Choosing what type of book club you'd like to create will help with creating a reasonable timeline for bringing your book club into fruition. There are two types of book clubs - online and location based. Let's talk about the differences, along with the pros and cons, for both.

Online Book Clubs are great because they are very convenient. Most people are computer savvy and already spend a lot of time online via Facebook, Twitter, blogs and other social media websites. Having social media outlets are truly a blessing and allow us to interact with people that we otherwise may not have met.

When setting up an online book club, there are many creative options for conducting meetings. Some book clubs use Twitter, blogs, Yahoo groups, Facebook, email threads, chat rooms and so forth to accomplish this. The great thing about creating an online book club is that people do not have to physically meet at a specific location. This can cost money and time for an individual, especially if the book club meets at a restaurant. With the exception of meeting in a chat room, members are able to contribute to the conversation at their leisure, and read everyone's thoughts regarding that month's book.

Some readers may be too shy to join a location based book club, but still want to discuss interesting books with people that appreciate great literature. Others don't have schedules that allow for formal meetings. For some, the expense of being a part of a location based book club may be too much. These are all sound reasons why online book clubs are so successful. An added bonus of creating an online book club is that you have the means to converse with people all over the world about your favorite books.

When creating an online book club, you must understand the amount of work involved. The first step of creating an online book club is to develop a website, blog, or group. You will need to set aside time for the upkeep of these online entities and will need to either be computer savvy or willing to learn. Creating guidelines can be a tricky. Online groups are generally more laidback than local groups, making it difficult to know when to cut inactive members. It's important that you keep order without creating so many guidelines that people lose interest in participating. People join online book clubs for the convenience and don't usually expect an overabundance of rules. Because the members are located in various parts of the country, it may be difficult to physically get everyone together for meet and greets. However, planning and attending reunions will bring your online group closer.

If you feel that you are internet savvy and can handle the responsibilities of an online book club, I say go for it!

Open vs. Closed Membership

You should decide if you're going to have an open or closed membership before you begin recruiting members. Open membership means that you're allowing people from the community to join your book club. This can easily be done by posting the information regarding your book club on various social websites or locations around your city i.e. libraries, grocery stores, college campuses.

The benefits of choosing an open membership are: your book club will be diverse because it will attract a variety of people that love to read, which will also make your book discussions richer. You don't have to question the reason why they are joining. Sometimes when inviting members into book clubs it can be difficult for them to stick with the guidelines because they get too comfortable and can decide that certain rules do not apply to them. Most people that join book clubs from the outside understand what they are getting themselves into and will generally stick with the program. Opening your book club to others can also create a great resource for yourself and your members as far as their job or skills are concerned. This could benefit the book club further down the line.

One of the cons of allowing open enrollment is that it may take more time for your book club to become cohesive. In time, your book club will become like a second family for you. We'll talk more about how to maintain your book club in chapter 5.

When starting a book club having a closed membership means that you would prefer to recruit members. This generally means that only current members can invite new members to join. By having a closed membership, book clubs have more control over the selection of potential members. This helps new members assimilate into the club more easily and ensures they are a good fit. Because of this, the group tends to be more intimate.

Closed membership can also mean that you're reached your capacity and no longer will be taking new members at this time.

One small drawback to having a closed membership is the lack of diversity within your group. Book clubs with closed membership are often comprised of friends within the same age group that share similar life experiences. The fun part of discussing a book is that everyone offers a different opinion based on their life journey. When the group is only comprised of people of a specific age, with similar backgrounds, the discussions can fall flat.

If you decide to have a closed membership, make an attempt at diversity by inviting readers from different age groups.

Setting a Criteria for Membership

Your book club is only as strong as your members. It is imperative that you set membership criteria to attract the type of members that will best fit your book club's mission and purpose.

There are seven key questions you should ask potential members. These questions will give insight into how certain individuals will fit into your book club. If you receive an answer that concerns you, email that person directly and ask for clarification. Explain your book club vision to make sure they fully understand what it will mean to be a part of your group. Dependent upon their answers, you may need to ask follow up questions.

Note: *You still need to take their personality into consideration, which you can't always gauge from these questions. You should think of other important questions that you can add to the list. We'll talk about how to gather all of this information later on in this chapter.*

Key Questions You Should Ask

Which genres do you like to read?
This will tell you if the potential member will be content reading the type of genres that your book club does. This could also be a chance for your book club to actually try new genres.

How many books do you read per month for enjoyment?

This is an important question because you want to know if they are avid readers and if they have time in their schedule to finish the required reading.

Do you feel that you'll be able to participate in meetings on a regular basis?

This will allow you to gauge whether or not the potential member will be able to commit to coming to meetings on a regular basis. By asking this question you will be sending the message that you expect them to attend the majority of the meetings and also participate in the discussion.

How much time do you feel that you have for yourself outside of your obligations?

This question will let you know if the potential member's obligations could possibly get in the way of them participating in book club meetings regularly.

Would you be willing to help plan events?

This question will help the potential member to explain to you what their expectations are if they were to join your book club. This will also help determine whether they are willing to grow with the book club as it moves forward.

Why would you like to join our book club?

This question will help the potential member express to you their interest in joining the book club in their own words and also help you gauge if there are serious about joining.

What do you hope to gain from joining our book club?

This question will help the potential member to explain to you what their expectations are if they were to join your book club and also help you to see if they are willing to grow as the book club move forward.

Optional Questions

- Who's your favorite author?

- What is your favorite book?

- What is your marital status?

- Do you have any children?

- What is your age range?

- What is your occupation?

- Do you have any hobbies?

- Would you like to share anything else about yourself?

Typical Information Gathering

- Name

- Email address

- Contact number (I think cell numbers are best)

- Address (only if you need it)

- How to create a membership application

Recruiting Members

Recruiting members for your book club can be easier than you think. I actually obtained forty-one members within eighteen months by using an online social event calendar. The online calendar allowed me to post information about my book club meetings. Interested parties saw the information and came to the meetings. Facebook and Twitter can also be utilized to attract potential members.

Word of mouth is a wonderful and free way to spread the word about your book club and your events. Talk to your friends, co-workers, and family members who are avid readers. Ask them to speak with their friends about your book club.

Place flyers, postcards, or business cards in book stores, libraries, hair salons, or any other establishments that may attract readers. Always have flyers on hand to pass out to readers you may happen to bump into by chance.

If you have any book signings in your area, ask the attendees if they belong to a book club. If not, hand them a flyer and encourage them to contact you if they are interested in joining. You can also ask other book club presidents to spread the word for you. Book Clubs that have reached their capacity are usually more than willing to direct potential members to alternate book clubs. This is also a good way to network and develop relationships with other groups.

So now that you have your potential members together. Let's prepare for your first meet & greet.

Preparing for Your First Meet & Greet

I highly recommend making the first gathering with your potential book club members a meet & greet. This will help everyone get to know one another and will be a wonderful opportunity to gather ideas. Make plans with the majority of your members in mind. As long as the majority of your members agree with what you'd like to do with the book club, keep your desired direction. Those who absolutely do not agree with your vision will remove themselves from the group.

Decide Where to Hold Your Meet & Greet

Find a neutral place to hold your meet and greet. This is especially helpful if you've invited people you've never met. Having a discussion over lunch, dinner, or drinks will help stir up a conversation and put everyone at ease.

Create an Evite or Send Invitations

Send out an Evite for everyone to reply to so that you can print out a record of who RSVP and so that others will know how much food to bring if you are requiring everyone to bring a dish.

Create Talking Points and an Itinerary

The first thing that you should do is to go back and gather your responses to *Exercise #1 Thinking it Through*, which is located in chapter one. Your answers will help you to create talking points for your meet & greet, which will assist you with creating an itinerary. This would also be a great opportunity to get feedback from others by engaging them in to a conversation after you discuss each point that you're bringing up. If you approach the group in this manner it will make them feel included in how the book club will operate, on some level, and not that they are being dictated to. You do have to keep in mind that the book club may be your baby but you have to learn that it really does take many people to create a book club. Be open to hear other ideas, which may be good for now or possibly later. Record the meeting or designate someone to take notes.

Choose One or Two Ice Breaker Games

Icebreaker games are really fun and can help your guests get to know one another. The games will help your guests feel at ease and will set the tone for your meeting. You can do a search online for great ideas on icebreaker games. Have small prizes or books available for the winners.

Pre-select Books for the First Two Book Club Meetings

Try to select books based on the feedback you've already received from application forms or the seven key questions. Do your homework and make sure the books you've chosen are readily available for purchase either in a book store or online. Be sure that you give your members enough time to purchase and read the book prior to your book club meeting.

Be Prepared for Extra Guests

Have extra membership forms available at the meet &
greet. Generally people will bring others with them that
may be interested in joining the book club.

Create a Sign in Sheet

Create a sign in sheet with all of your member's names
on it so they can sign in at the beginning of the meeting.
This will also help you verify the information that you
have already gathered. Be sure you ask for their address
so that you can send everyone a thank you card after the
meeting.

Preparing for Your First Book Club Meeting

For the most part, preparing for your first book club
meeting requires the same steps listed in the previous
section, Preparing for Your First Meet & Greet. It's really
your choice how formal or informal you'd like your
meeting to be. The steps above are just a guideline to get
you started until you find a happy medium on how you'd
like your meetings to go.

More importantly, it's essential that you know how to
facilitate a book club discussion. So we're going to go over
some essential steps on how to conduct an effective
discussion in *Chapter 5: Maintaining a Successful Book
Club Meeting.*

CHAPTER 3 EXERCISE

CREATING YOUR BOOK CLUB FOUNDATION

The following questions will help you to begin thinking about what type of book club that you want and also so you can begin to create a timeline in order to stay on track with your targeted launch date for your book club.

1. Which type of book club would you like to create and why?

2. Will you choose to have open or closed membership?

3. Make a list of potential members.

4. List the criteria in order for potential members to join your book club.

5. Create a reasonable timeline to keep track while creating your book club, including preparing for your meet & greet and initial book club meeting. *You should include tasks, deadlines and who will be responsible for completing the tasks on the timeline.*

CHAPTER 3 NOTES

CHAPTER 3 NOTES

CHAPTER 4

CREATING PEACE WITH BYLAWS

Overview

When creating a book club it's always a good idea to create bylaws. Bylaws are very important to have in place because it lets everyone know how the book club will operate. Having bylaws in place also cuts down on miscommunication and misinterpretation between members on how the book club will operate and decisions that has been recently been implemented. Bylaws are also a great reference point to direct new members to as well in order to not have to constantly repeat book club specifics.

Objectives

- Discuss why bylaws are important to have in place for your book club

- The eight key points that should be covered in your bylaws

The Importance of Developing Bylaws

There are various reasons why bylaws should be in place when creating your book club, instead of waiting until an issue presents itself. Here are the most important reasons why you should create bylaws for your book club:

- Protects the vision of your book club.

- Sets the tone and provides normalcy for your book club.

- Provides guidance for decision making regarding your book club.

- Allows book club to be proactive instead of being reactive to potentially unpleasant situations.

- Provides a reference for present and future members to refer back to.

- Helps to decrease misinterpretation and/or miscommunication amongst book club members.

It's easy to think that bylaws are not necessary because your book club is new, may not have officers, or not involved in community service etc. but all book clubs should have bylaws in place from the beginning.

Bylaws can be very simple or as in depth as you want them to be. Bylaws are a written document that basically helps everyone to understand how the book club will operate. Bylaws are great to have in place, especially when you had new members to your book club. Trust me, after you've repeated the same answers several times you'll definitely wish you had you bylaws written down and available to hand to your members, instead of reciting them by heart.

When making important decisions in regards to your book club its best that you have the final decisions in writing so there aren't any misinterpretations or misunderstandings. It's really hard for anyone to argue the details of the bylaws that were agreed upon by book club members versus someone misinterpreting what was said, which can cause a lot of confusion. You should think of creating bylaws as a way to be proactive versus being reactive.

Eight Essential Bylaw Elements

Bylaws should include all of the details that encompass your book club. It's best to have some ideas of what you would like to place in your bylaws before you introduce them to your book club members. Once you have a good idea of what you'd like to cover in your bylaws you should then ask for suggestions from your members. By having your members involved in creating your bylaws, they will more than likely be more acceptable to the terms. You definitely need to have your members 'buy in' to the bylaws in order to keep them relevant. It will also help your members understand how important the book club is and why it's important to have guidelines in place.

It's best to create bylaws when you first create your book club with just a few members involved, instead of when you have 10-15 members. Generally, smaller groups are easier to manage when making decisions because there are not so many opinions that you'll have to deal with.

Mission Statement

A mission statement basically states the reason why your book club exists. It sets the tone for how your book club will operate and also how your vision will be carried out. Your mission statement will also help you make decisions regarding your book club in order to succeed in reaching your goals as a book club.

When creating your mission statement here are a few things you should keep in mind:

- Think about your vision for your book club.

- State who and how your mission will affect the people involved.

- State how your book club intends on carrying out your vision.

- State what type of services your book club will provide, if any.

Refer back to your answers to the Chapter 2 Exercise to help you create your mission statement.

Book Club Officer Positions and Descriptions

State each book club officer position to be held in your book club. You should describe each position's responsibilities, how long the member will hold their position and the election/appointment process. Not all book clubs have appointed officers, which is a personal choice. It may be better to hold off on appointing officers until you have your book club established. This will give you a chance to figure out who your devoted members are and which positions they would be great at. Take your time when choosing your officers. Make sure they attend meetings on a regular basis and are reliable.

You should also state if your position as the book club president will always remain the same or if the position will rotate to others after a certain amount of time. If you will be holding an officer's meeting, you should state how often you will meet and other specifics.

Membership Requirements

All book clubs have specific requirements when considering new members. You should be very clear when describing your expectations for new members so that they know what to expect before they contact your book club. This will help filter out the potential members that may not be a fit for your book club. Before you begin to set your membership requirements, be sure to take the following into consideration:

Open Membership
How often you will take in new members. State the maximum amount of members for your book club. State if there's a probationary period.

Closed Membership
State if your membership will be by invitation only or closed altogether.

Gender
State if your book club will be co-ed or single gendered.
Reading Material

You should state the genres your book club reads and any other qualifications unique to your book club.

Book Club Meeting Specifics

State the following particulars about your book club meetings:

State the time, place, and date the meetings will take place.

Members should be aware of the specifics of when meetings should take place so that they are better prepared to work around their schedules. Do not change the dates or times of meeting unless it's necessary. Otherwise you will not have good attendance at your meetings

Describe how your book club meetings will be facilitated and the facilitator's responsibilities

You want to be as specific as possible with describing the responsibilities of the facilitator and what requirements the facilitators has to meet in order to host a meeting i.e. Do they have to be a member for a certain amount of time? Will you require members to attend a number of consecutive meetings before the member can facilitate?

Describe your book selection process

Will you allow one member to recommend a book or have everyone vote from 2-3 books? Will you choose all of the books for the entire year or choose a few at a time? Are there specific genres that your book club will choose to read or exclude?

If you plan to host authors you should list how soon you'd be able to host the author in respect to obtaining the book. You should make sure you give yourself time to purchase and receive the book in a timely manner so that your members ready to discuss the book with the author.

* *Author Tip **

From time to time you may get an author that will contact you at the last minute requesting a hosted book club meeting. Most times it's because the author is planning to be in your area and discovered your group at the last minute. It's okay to say no if this is not feasible for your group. It's really hard to gather members together on a non-book club day or to change your book selection within 30 days in order to accommodate an author's request. If the author is appearing in your city it may be easier to show support by attending the event the author is due to appear at, if it's open to the public. You can also choose to read the author's book at a later date and have them discuss their book in person, on a conference call, through video conference or Twitter. It's really important that you keep your book club meetings as consistent as possible so that your members know what to expect and can plan ahead accordingly.

Author Expenses

When hosting a book club meeting for an author, be sure to discuss if there's any expenses that the book club will pay for and if a gift will be involved. You should also state how this expense will be paid.

You should also decide how many authors per year you will invite to your meeting if there's an expense involved. This will help you plan ahead and increase dues or plan fundraisers in order to help pay for the expenses, if any.

If food is going to be provided you should state who is to provide or pay for it.

In general, if you hold your book club meetings at a restaurant, each member should be responsible for paying for their own meal.

If you choose to host meetings in a member's home, you should decide if the facilitator is responsible for purchasing and preparing the meal or will all the members pitch in and bring a dish. I believe that it's best to spread the expense of the meal and have each member bring a dish. You can either plan a menu or do a potluck. You may want to think about using a portion of your dues to cover costs as well.

Decide which month your annual planning meeting will be held.

All book clubs should really hold an annual planning/business meeting. If your book club is involved with a lot of events or projects you will probably need to hold business meetings more often. Some book clubs may choose to use a portion of their monthly book club meeting time to talk about book club business as well. It really just depends on how active your book club is.

You should discuss your budget, dues, fundraisers and community service project ideas (if applicable), upcoming literary events (either that your group will attend or coordinate), discuss any revisions for the bylaws, book club concerns that you or your members may have and any other book club business.

Dues

Collecting dues can be helpful to pay for activities and to operate your book club. It's not necessary to take up dues if you do not have a good reason to do so. Either way you should have a brief statement to cover dues in your by-laws.

Examples of typical book club expenses: website fees, community service project expenses, birthday gifts etc.

Answer the following questions when stating information about the dues:

Why are you collecting dues?

State the reasons for taking up dues. State specifically what the dues will cover. If dues are not going to be collected, state just that and also that the book club reserves the right to collect dues at anytime with proper notice.

How much are annual dues?

You should state how much your dues will be and how often they will be collected. It's important that you do not take up dues just because. Assess your obligations carefully and then determine the appropriate amount of dues that you'll need to collect. Remember that being a book club member can become expensive when you take into consideration the cost of books and food on top of monthly dues. If you see that the dues are too expensive for your group to pay you should go back and reassess the amount and see if it can be readjusted.

How will dues be collected?

State the amount of dues per month for each member, what forms of payments are acceptable, and how often they will be collected. You should also address what will happen for non-payment i.e. grace periods, exclusion from the book club etc.

Who will be responsible for collecting dues?

State the person who will be responsible for receiving and keeping track of the dues.

TaNisha's Pearl of Wisdom

The purpose for taking up dues is to help assist the book club's daily operations NOT to give members the option to miss meeting! You may need to reiterate this point from time to time. If you have a faithful member that is experiencing financial difficulties you should try to work out an agreement with the member or consider waiving the dues until they are able to get on their feet. You shouldn't allow money to get in the way of losing a great member. Assess each case individually and then come up with a solution.

Code of Conduct

A code of conduct (COC) is a set of rules and regulations informing members how they should conduct themselves as a representative of the book club. A COC can include anything that will help protect the integrity of your book club and keep the relationship between your members intact.

TaNisha's Pearl of Wisdom

It's not okay to allow disruptive members to continue on in your book club. If members grow tired of their foolishness, you risk losing your faithful members. Remove this member from your book club as peacefully and as soon as possible.

Community Service/Social Event

State the community service projects and/or social outings that your book club will partake in on a regular basis. List the logistics for each of these entities.

Review of Bylaws

In order to keep your bylaws current and relevant you should review your bylaws on an annual basis. Bylaws should be adjusted to best fit your book club and will need to be changed from time to time to support the book club's vision and mission statement.

It's really important that you are very specific when creating your bylaws. Take your time and include your book club members in helping you create the bylaws so that they not only understand them but will be more than willing to abide by them.

CHAPTER 4 EXERCISE

DEVELOPING YOUR MISSION STATEMENT & BYLAWS

The questions below are intended to help you create a mission statement. You should think about your questions to the answers that you provided in the Chapter 2 Exercise and really think about what you want your book club to stand for and how you plan on accomplishing those things.

When creating a rough draft of your bylaws, go through this chapter and write down the different components down, regardless if you plan on implementing them in your book club or now. Write down your ideas and then present those ideas to your members so that you can discuss them together.

1. Complete your mission statement based on your answers in Chapter 2 and the guidance in the mission statement section in this chapter.

2. Write out a rough draft of your bylaws to present to your book club members. Finalize your bylaws once you receive feedback from your members.

CHAPTER 4 NOTES

CHAPTER 4 NOTES

CHAPTER 5

STEPS TO MAINTAINING A SUCCESSFUL BOOK CLUB

Overview

Now that your book club is established, the work has just begun! Maintaining a book club can be challenging but worth it. In this chapter we're going to go over some key elements on how to keep your book club in good shape.

Objectives

- Discuss the three major responsibilities of a facilitator

- Learn steps to facilitating an effective book club discussion

- Learn how to facilitate an annual planning meeting

Steps to Facilitating a Book Club Meeting

In order to create a cohesive book club, there must be some structure. Learning how to facilitate an effective book club meeting and discussion is necessary in order to create a comfortable atmosphere where everyone can enjoy the book discussion and one another.

Having structure for your book club doesn't mean that you have to have a lot of rules. It's just a way for your members to know what to expect during a meeting. It's important that you come up with a standard way of facilitating your book club meeting.

Facilitator Responsibilities

A facilitator is the book club meeting host and basically has three major roles: To choose the book of the month selection (for most book clubs), host the book club meeting, and facilitate the book discussion.

Book of the Month Selections

Most book clubs allow the facilitator to select the book of the month, while others may decide to bring a few selections and then take a vote. It's important that the facilitator either choose the book or bring in the books to choose from so that the person is in charge of that particular meeting from the beginning. This will cut down on all of the confusion with who's in charge. If you have a lot of members you can choose to have more than one facilitator during each meeting in order to keep all of your members involved. It's really important that you allow your members to choose the books after the first 2-3 meetings. This will give you a good idea which genres work well with your group. Generally the first year is the hardest when choosing books because individually, some members may like specific genres but as a group that particular genre may not work out.

Tips on Selecting Books
- Make sure you download a preview of the book so that you can read a few chapters of the book before you select it. (You can do this on most online book store websites either via pdf or an Ereader)

- Select authors that you may not be familiar with. Book clubs are about exposing yourself to books that you may not have picked up on your own. Most book clubs start out choosing authors that they are more familiar with but you should also choose authors that you do not know as well. (Be sure you download a preview of the book by the author)

- Make sure that the book is available for purchase.

- Check other book club websites to see what they are reading.

- Read reliable reviews by other book clubs and reviewers to see what they are saying about the book.

- Keep at least 3-4 months of book selections available to your members at all times. This will help members to prepare for upcoming book club meetings well in advance. Members also read faster than others. So this will help your members move ahead to the next book.

Book Club Meeting Host

The facilitator is normally the one to decide the specifics for the book club meeting. They choose if the meeting will take place in their home or in a restaurant and what the menu will consist of, unless you're meeting in a restaurant. The facilitator is also in charge of the ice breaker games if applicable. All of this information should be relayed to the president or whoever is in charge with helping with the book club meetings.

Tips for Planning Meetings

- Make sure that your book club meeting time and date stay the same so that everyone knows when to expect the book club meeting.

- Make sure you keep in touch with the facilitator and set a deadline for book club meeting details so that you can give your members notice.

- If your members need to switch months be sure it's not within 4 weeks of the meeting. By that time the members would have already began reading the book selection.

- Make sure you start your meetings on time. You may want to consider separating your meal from your book discussion if you meet out in restaurants so your discussion isn't interrupted. Also, if some of your members do not like the restaurant or running late it will allow them to join you at a specific time to discuss the book only. Some book clubs may use the meal time to go over book club business, to socialize, or to play ice breaker games.

Book Discussion Facilitator

The facilitator is also responsible for leading the book discussion. Their main role is to initiate the book discussion questions and to make sure the discussion stays on track. Good books are generally relatable, which will cause members to talk about their experiences. This is fine to do because you learn a lot about one another, which will make you closer as a group. The facilitator should know when to move the discussion along in order to keep everyone engaged and so that the discussion doesn't turn into a discussion that has nothing to do about the book.

Tips for Preparing for Book Discussions

- Get familiar with the discussion questions in the back of the book and choose the best questions or have your own questions ready.

- Don't be afraid to move the discussion along.

- Make sure everyone is engaged into the conversation. Encourage members to participate in the conversation by calling on them to answer specific questions.

Steps to Facilitating an Effective Book Club Discussion

In order to have an enjoyable discussion you must have engaging discussion questions. There's several different options how you can come up with book discussion questions.

Discussion Questions Provided in the Book

Some books will offer discussion questions in the back of the book, or on the author and/or publisher's website. Most book clubs find these questions to be very helpful to discuss books, especially if you have a new book club.

Developing Discussion Questions

Don't worry if there are no discussion questions available or choose books that only provide discussion questions. Instead, jot down thoughts and questions as you read the book and come up with questions on your own. Most times the best discussion questions are the ones that you think of on your own and not the questions provided in the back of the book. Readers tend to ask questions from books that either cause them to relate to or in opposition with the characters or a situation.

- Make sure that you ask open ended questions so that you will generate a discussion instead of a yes or no response.

- When discussing a book you may find that you're unable to ask all of the questions. This generally happens because the questions were so great that it provoked other members to ask even better questions or because the discussion ran into the ditch with conversations that had nothing to do with the book. This is why it's a great idea to have a facilitator for book discussions. The facilitator is responsible for making sure that the discussion doesn't get too far off track.

- You can also ask each member to write down 2-3 questions and then draw questions out of a bowl or jar. This will help the book club members stay engaged and also make them aware that they must read the book. If you pull a question that has already been discussed, discard it and then pull another one.

Discussion Participation

It's important that everyone has a chance to participate in the discussion. This may be hard to do if you're discussing a great book that everyone wants to talk about or if you have a large group. You may want to adopt a few rules if this is the case. Some book clubs use timers to keep track of how long book club members speak. Basically whoever holds the timer is the only one permitted to speak. The timer is set for 2-3 minutes (or however long you'd like to set it for), which will allow everyone the chance to speak. On the other hand, you may have some members that are shy or have very few words to say. Make sure you call on those members so they feel included in the conversation.

Playing ice breaker games at the beginning or throughout your meeting that pertains to the book selection can also make discussing the book fun as well. You can find icebreaker games online that can be adapted to book club activities.

Annual Planning Meetings

Every book club should schedule an annual planning meeting in order to plan ahead for the next year and to go over different components that make up the book club. One of the easiest ways to do this is to create an agenda in order cover different areas of your book club. You can easily do this by using the topics covered in your bylaws to create different talking points. You should also discuss next year's budget as well.

Budget

When discussing your budget you need to know what your income and expenses are. Be sure to gather your banks statements and expense reports so that you can go over them during your meeting. You should come to a consensus with your members on how to spend your book club's money, what expenses need to be covered based on upcoming projects and miscellaneous expenses. You need to select which fundraisers you'd like to do in order to generate income for the book club. Your book club dues should be discussed as well and determine if adjustments are needed.

Income
Your dues and money earned from fundraising should be recorded under your income.

Expenses
Any book club related bills should be recorded as a response i.e. website fees, event fees, author expenses, gifts etc. Anything that generates a bill or expense should be added as well such as expenses for community service projects.

Income and Expense Report Tip
Using an income and expense report spreadsheet in Excel that calculates is a great way to keep track of your

income and expenses. You can customize each of the items to fit your book club and tell if you're in the red or the green with your budget. You can find these types of spreadsheets for free by just doing an internet search. You can also customize this type of report when planning literary events to keep track of your expenses.

Mission Statement

Going over your mission statement can help keep your book club focused on setting goals for the next years. You always want to make decisions for your book club that supports your mission statement. Sometimes your book club's focus can change. This isn't necessarily a bad thing. You should consider adjusting your mission statement if you find that the book club's vision has changed.

Book Club Officers

If you have book club officers you should have them put together an annual report in regards to the various activities that they were responsible for. You should be holding meetings with your officers throughout the year but this would be a great time to go over everything regarding the book club with everyone. If your book club changes officers on a yearly basis this may be a good time to talk about nomination or appointment process as well.

New Membership

Your book club should discuss if the group will be taking in new members and what that process will be.

Some book clubs coordinate an annual or semi-annual new member meet & greet, which will need to be planned. Create a plan that works for your book club. Meet & greets can be an "all out" event or it can be as simple as inviting potential members to a member's home or a meet up at a restaurant during Happy Hour. Basically meet & greets can be done within any budget.

Book Club Meetings

You should begin to plan for next year's book club meetings by at least assigning facilitators. You may or may not be ready to choose books but this will at least get everyone enough time to begin thinking about a book to discuss during their month. Some book clubs plan their entire book selection for the year at one time and some choose just a few at a time. Choose what works for your book club.

If you host book club meetings for authors you should begin brainstorming and come up with a list of authors you'd like to attend your meeting. Be sure that you talk about any expenses that you'll cover for the authors and include them in your expense report. Keep in mind that you can also have authors attend your meeting via conference calls and Skype to save money.

Dues

You should always talk about your dues on an annual basis and discuss if there need to be any adjustments. If there is a need to increase the amount of dues you should bring this up to the group and give valid reasons why. If your book club members are struggling to pay dues you may need to consider decreasing your dues for the year.

You should also consider doing more fundraisers to compensate the decrease or cut back on some of the projects that you have planned for the upcoming year.

Community Service/Events

A discussion should take place in regards to which events you're book club would like to attend and plan; community projects that you'd like to participate in or coordinate; and also fundraisers you'd like to begin for the next year. If you're planning an event you should begin planning early by laying out a timeline soon and getting everyone involved by delegating duties.

Review of Bylaws

You should provide a copy of your bylaws to everyone to go over to see if there need to be any updates. You should all come to an agreement what need to be updated and the language. You should email the bylaws and have your members look over them prior to the meeting so they can propose any changes at the time of the meeting. Make sure you place at the bottom of your bylaws the month and year they were revised.

Personal Book Club Issues

If there are any personal issues that need to be resolved with the book club as a whole or with individual members the annual planning meeting is the perfect time to get everything out on the table. Anything that is said should be left in the meeting so that everyone can move on. All members should be able to express their feelings about the book club without any backlash. This part of the meeting should take place last for obvious reasons. ☺

Annual Planning Meeting Follow Ups

More than likely there will be a few follow ups that need to be done after your annual meeting. Make sure you set a deadline for the follow to be completed and when the group can expect to receive the follow ups so decisions can be made.

CHAPTER 5 EXERCISE

FACILITATING & ANNUAL PLANNING MEETINGS

It's time to think about how your book club meetings will be conducted. There is no right or wrong answer. This is your book club. What you find works in the beginning may need to be modified later on.

1. Visit the sections *How to Facilitate a Successful Book Club Meeting* and *Steps to Facilitating an Effective Book Club Discussion* and go over each of the points on how to facilitate and hold a discuss and start planning how your meetings will take shape and what the responsibilities will be for your facilitators.

2. Decide which meeting will be the month that you hold your annual book club planning meeting. *For example: My book club planning meeting is held in August because people are just coming off of vacation and school begins the day after our meeting takes place so naturally this is a meeting that books do not typically get read and attendance is low. The annual planning meeting is mandatory for all members to attend. Because we hold the meeting in August it also give us 4 months to gather further information to make the final decisions for the following year.*

CHAPTER 5 NOTES

CHAPTER 5 NOTES

CHAPTER 6

CREATE AN INTERNET PRESENCE FOR YOUR BOOK CLUB

Overview

Creating an internet presence for your book club is essential for many reasons. Several book clubs fail to create a website, which can make it difficult for authors, other book clubs and potential members to find them. In this chapter we're going to explore the different facets of a website and social media.

Objectives

- Discuss why book clubs should create an internet presence

- Discuss the different facets of creating book club website

- Discuss the benefits and drawbacks of social media websites

Why Book Clubs Should Create an Internet Presence

There's several thousands of book clubs that exist across the country but only a small percentage actually have an internet presence. An internet presence is essential because it creates a virtual address so that book clubs can be found by authors, publishing companies, fellow book clubs and potential members. Connecting to these entities are important for various reasons.

For author and publishing companies it's essential that they know where to find book clubs because it can make the difference whether authors and publishing companies are willing to do book signings in a specific city. Many of their decisions for book signings is determined on if they can initially locate local book clubs. Afterwards, the publishing company looks at how many people showed up at the book signing and the book sales, especially when considering that particular city for a potential book tour stop in the future. Because of the introduction of electronic readers, it's essential that book clubs and avid readers support authors when the visit their city by attending book signings and purchasing books in order to insure the author will visit again. If book clubs cannot be located, authors and publishing companies will be hesitant to place some cities as a book tour stop.

Connecting with fellow book clubs in or close to your city can be very beneficial if both book clubs want to partner together on community service projects, literary events or travel together. Supporting fellow book clubs can prove beneficial for your book club if you're able to locate them.

If your book club is looking for potential members an internet presences is very helpful because it allows the potential member to gather information about the book club prior to contacting you. This also helps book club members to direct potential members to the website instead giving out email address or phone numbers to people they do not know and also with not having to repeat the same information several times to different people

Having a website is major benefit for your book club members as well. Being able to place your book of the month selections, meetings and other items on your website will cut down on repeating yourself by making essential information available to them and also cut down on constantly emailing the information out to them.

If your book club coordinate events or participate in community service projects or fundraiser you should definitely have a website in place so that people can have the information available to them. Temporary event planning pages such as Evite, Eventbrite etc. work better if they are embedded into a page or associated with a website, instead of a temporary website page that is created by these event planning websites because you can include much more details about the event. If your book club coordinates an annual event you can also create a permanent page on your website so that people will be aware far in advance when the date will be coming around.

Hopefully you get the idea why having an internet presence, particularly a website, is really important to a book club. Now let's discuss what should be present on a website.

How to Create a Book Club Website

Establishing a website is the most practical way to create an internet presence for book clubs. People tend to be intimidated with creating a website and do not want to bother having to maintain it. Most times the work is creating the website but once you create it not much changes on the website, unless you decide to place time sensitive information on most of the pages.

Nowadays, creating websites are really simple and very cheap. Because book clubs tend to not have a lot of money, it's important to shop around for the best website server with the best price. You can choose to pay someone to create and maintain your website or you can be economical and create your own.

If you're considering hiring a website developer, you should consider the cost involved and if you are going to choose to have the developer maintain the website or maintain it on your own. You should be sure to ask plenty of questions including the following: What are the monthly or yearly website hosting fees? How many website pages that the price will include? How much will it cost to add and/or update the pages? Do you have the option of owning your own domain independently from the website itself and monthly maintenance fees? Will you be able to maintain your own website?

In this chapter, we're going to talk about how to create your own website on a limited budget; how to find website servers for the novice website developer; how to secure your domain; and the essential and optional pages that should be present on your website.

Securing a Website Server and Domain Name

Website Server

A website server is what is known to host a website. The website server is what delivers a person to a particular website on request by using the Hypertext Transfer Portal (http). Choosing a website server can be a daunting task but it's important that you shop around and compare different website server features and prices. You also want to look to see if a novice web designer like yourself will be able to handle creating a website. Servers that have a drag and drop feature are very easy to use for someone that has no experience creating a website. In order to not show favoritism to one website server over another, I would suggest that you do an internet search for *free websites*.

Before you choose a website server try a few of them out before making a final decision. Most website servers have a free or trial version that will allow you to practice creating a website.

Domain Name

A domain name is an internet identifier that directs an internet user to a specific website aka a website address. When choosing a website server, I would suggest that you choose a website server that will allow you to purchase a domain name separately with the option to use your domain name on their website for free or at a low cost. This is an important feature if you ever want to switch to another server or have a professional web designer create a website for your book club so that you do not have to change the domain name or not have to pay a large fee to maintain the domain.

If you choose to purchase your domain at the time you secure your website, you are subject to pay more per year than if you were to purchase the domain name separately. Most free websites will allow you to use your own domain name for free (depending on the host plan you purchase – if that's a factor), where your only expense would be to pay for the domain name on a yearly basis. Most domains cost anywhere from $0.99 - $20.00 per year. You will also need to purchase some other security options to help protect your contact information. This would be required on any website that allows you to purchase a domain name.

When choosing a company to purchase your domain name, you should pay close attention to the regular price if the domain site offers a special rate at the time you purchase your domain name. There are some domain websites that will reel in unsuspecting customers with low rates in the beginning and will then charge extremely high renewal fees later on. So don't necessarily pay attention to the sales but what the regular yearly rates are instead. If you choose to purchase more than one domain, I would suggest that you stick to one company so you can keep track of them all in one place. If you find a domain company that offers a cheaper yearly rate you can always choose to transfer your domain to another company for a low fee.

All domain sights will have you do a search to make sure that the name that you want is not already taken. Make sure that you lock in the name that you want and make sure that you are satisfied with that name before you purchase it. If your book club's name is long try to figure out a simple website address that people can remember. *Example: KC Girlfriends Book Club www.kcgbc.com*

Website Pages

When building a website there are a few pages that should be present. These pages may need minor updates from time to time but for the most part most pages will be complete once you figure out what content to place on it.

Essential Website Pages
When creating a website you should always include the following five pages and content listed:

Home Page

This page should be the introduction to who your book club is and where you're located. You can also include brief information on how your book club was established and your book of the month selection.

About Us Page

This page should go into more details about the history of your book club. You can also choose to talk about some of your book club's favorite authors and/or books, and introduce your book club members.

Membership Page

This page should describe how someone can become a member of your book club. You should include as many details as possible about the membership process. Creating some type of online membership application is great for gathering information about the potential member. This will help you determine if the person will be a good fit for your book club. Even if your book club has a closed membership you should state that on the website.

Contact Us Page

You should embed a contact form or give your contact information on this particular page. The benefit of using a contact form is that it's easy to keep track where your emails are coming from. Most websites also store old emails on your website server just in case you accidently delete an email.

Optional Website Pages

There are quite a few optional pages that you can choose to incorporate onto your website. When place website pages on your website be sure to know go overboard. Otherwise your website will become cluttered and busy.

Members Page

This particular page can be used to introduce your book club members. You can also place a short bio for each member and fun facts.

Members Only Page

Some website servers allow you to incorporate a password protected page on your website. This is a great way to include information that you do not want the general public to see about book club business but make it accessible to book club members in one location.

Book Review Submission Page

If your book club will be taking book review submissions you should include a page on your website that lists all the guidelines.

Book of the Month Selection Page

People always want to know what book clubs are reading, especially other book clubs and potential members. Book selections also help authors to gauge which genres your book club read.

Event or Calendar Page

If you're book club is really active or coordinate a lot of events you should create an event page or embed a calendar into your website. This will keep everyone up to date with what you're book club is doing.

Blog Page

A blog is a great way to get people to interact with your book club and to visit your website on a regular basis. Keeping people up to date on what your book club is currently doing, book reviews, sharing random thoughts and asking questions that will engage people to comment are great ways to let everyone know that your book club is still active. With blogs you must submit entries on a regular basis.

Revenue Options

Can you believe that your website can make you money? If you're especially internet savvy earning revenue through your website may be the way to go! In order to do this, you will need to set up a PayPal account so that you can receive credit card payments.

Ad Space

Renting advertisement space to authors and other literary entities on your website can earn your book club money! Low advertising costs can bring in big bucks and become a great fundraiser. Going the extra step to create a newsletter that can be emailed or shared on social media websites is also a plus.

Book Store Affiliate Programs

You can also become an online book store affiliate via Amazon and other websites and embed a book store onto your website. Placing your book club's book of the month selections in the book store is easy and can earn you money as well. If your book club purchases their books online, you should have them purchase their books through your Amazon book store. Even if the person does not purchase any of the books in your store but purchases something else, even a non –book item, you will still earn money. You can also place a widget on any page of your website as well.

Fundraiser Page

If your group participates in fundraisers for community service projects or for your book club you should consider placing your current fundraiser information on your website.

Meta Tags

Meta tags are keywords that help someone find information by performing an internet search. Meta tags or Meta keywords are HTML codes that are placed in the header on a webpage, after the title page. These specific words or 'tags' are not viewable by people visiting your website like they are when you visit blogs.

You should be able to find a space to place your Meta tags under the settings on your website server. You want to place various groups of words as a Meta tag that you think people would use if they were trying to perform an internet search to find your book club but didn't know your book club's name. The more tags you add, the more likely your book club will come up at the top of an internet search. You should perform random checks on different search engines to see what number your book club is on the search results. If you do not place Meta tags in your settings it can make it very difficult for people to find your book club. If you see that your book club is lower than number four on the search result list, you should add more Meta tags in your settings. You should add as many variations of Meta tags as possible. Another thing that will bring your book club's name up on search results is having others mention your book club in articles, on websites, Twitter etc. Always place your website information on articles etc to make it easier for people to find your website.

For my book club, KC Girlfriends Book Club I have placed many keywords in the Meta tag setting so that when someone is searching for book clubs in the area we will come up on the top of the list without that person knowing the name of our group.

Meta Tag Examples: Book Clubs in Missouri, Book Clubs in Kansas, Book Clubs in Kansas City, MO, Book Clubs in Kansas City, KS, Book Clubs, Book Clubs in the Kansas City Metro, Book Clubs in the Midwest, KC Girlfriends etc.

You should also place a short website description on the setting page as well. This is what a person will typically see once the result of the web search is displayed. The description should include your book club's location, when it was established. You only need to include up to 3 sentences in the description. This can be helpful so that the person knows they have found the right website and book club.

Social Media

Social media is a great way to interact with others in the literary industry in real time. It's really important that you do not substitute creating a website in exchange for a social media profile. Social media accounts should be used in addition to your website only.

Using Facebook and Twitter is a great way to create a rapport with your favorite authors and to connect with fellow book clubs and readers. Both of these social media websites are not the best way for interested individuals to learn everything about your book club that you may want them to know. Facebook is a great way to promote events or your interests but it doesn't connect you to everyone that could possibly be interested in attending your event, especially if they do not have a Facebook account. For both Facebook and Twitter, status updates are sporadic as far as who sees them because everyone is never on either one at the same time.

Twitter is more challenging to use but it's a great way to send messages or information about something or nothing at all. Twitter can be highly affective but only works if you use it and interact with others on a regular basis. Twitter can be used to hold book discussion chats and keep everyone updated on various events as they are happening. The trick to Twitter is that you have to learn what to say and how to say it in 140 characters or less that will make others not only read and respond but also share i.e. retweet the message to others to make it go viral i.e. share with their list of followers and then their followers share it with others etc.

You can embed both Facebook and Twitter widgets into your website so that people are aware that they can connect with your group via both social media websites. If you're going to add the widgets onto your website make sure you are constantly using them. Underused accounts can give the indication that your book club isn't active or hard to connect to online.

Another great social network to join is Goodreads. Goodreads is a great way to share what you're reading with others and also offer book reviews to people that are following your book club. Most of your Goodreads friends tend to comment on book reviews or the books that you're currently reading. The interaction is a little bit slower but it offers a great environment to interact with avid readers. You can also join some of the groups and discussion boards as well on a variety of literary topics and interests. All three social media websites allows you to connect with one another so that you're able to post one time and have your update post to all three accounts at one time.

Other social media communities worth mentioning are Instagram and Pinterest. You should look them up to see if there are something that you would like to try out to create a social media presence as well.

Although creating a website may be overwhelming in the beginning, you'll definitely see the benefits of creating an internet and social media presence. Take your time and do your research and then select the correct internet presences for your book club.

There's not exercise for Chapter 6. Just do your research on website servers and domains. ☺

CHAPTER 6 NOTES

CHAPTER 6 NOTES

CHAPTER 7

CREATING BOOK REVIEW STANDARDS

Overview

It's quite natural for book clubs to be approached by authors or publishing companies to read and review books. Providing book reviews not only helps to create a presence for a book club but it also helps authors and publishing companies market books. It's really important that book clubs not only know how to write reviews but also insure that as a group all of the reviews are consistent, unbiased and objective. This chapter will help you create a book review standard based on what you feel are the most important elements in a book.

Objectives

- Learn the importance of creating book review standards for your book club.

- Learn five important book review elements that you should consider while creating book review standards

- Learn how to offer book reviews and the information you should provide

Please note: this chapter is meant to help you come up with your own book review standards based on what you feel are important elements that makes a great book. Please feel free to create your own standards based on what you read in this chapter. If you choose to use some or the same exact standards, please know that you must notify me and ask permission to use the standards. You cannot change the wording and must site that you used the KC Girlfriends Book Club Review Standards on all reviews. This review standard is copy written. Thanks for your cooperation. ☺

Why the KC Girlfriends Book Club Review Standard Was Created

Once the KC Girlfriends Book Club was up and running again, we created an internet presence, which quite naturally attracted authors that wanted my book club to review their books. In the beginning, it was easy for me to keep up with the book review requests. But soon after I created the KC Girlfriends Book Club Radio Show the demand for providing book reviews grew, which caused me to enlist the help of my book club members.

During a panel discussion on my radio show about the book review process, I came up with the idea of creating a book review standard for my members. I didn't want the book review standards to silence the voice my members but to insure that all of us were taking the same elements into consideration, while reviewing books. Also, none of my book club members had previous experience with reviewing books so it also helped to have a book review process in place so that the turnaround time was speedy.

The Challenge

Quite simply, one of the challenges with book reviews is that they can be very subjective. Without having some type of standard in place, book reviews will remain to be all over the map. Some of the common issues with book reviews are: too much information or spoilers are given away; some reviewers get way too personal and attack the author; and some reviewers simply do not review the book at all or do not say exactly why a book received a specific rating.

I knew that my book club members had no experience with providing book reviews and I wanted to make sure that we were looking at the same elements in the books that we read and that they were not only able to give their honest opinion but justified why they felt the way they did regarding the book by keeping the specified elements in mind. It was also important that I set up some type of process on how the reviews would be written and submitted.

The Discussion

The first step in resolving our book review dilemma was to identify the important elements that my book club felt should be represented in the type of books that we read. Because we are not professional book reviewers we felt that our book reviews should be reflective of what an avid reader would look for in a great book. We basically wanted to focus on all aspects of what would attract a reader to purchase the book, along with the storyline, character development and editing process.

Because book reviews are based on a five star rating my book club members and I came up with the five most important elements that should be represented in every book. Based on those five elements I had to figure out exactly how each of those elements would be represented in the book review standards and how it would be weighed in order to figure out the star rating. Once we agreed on the five elements, I was ready to move on to figuring out how to create a process that would offer an objective review.

The Solution

The second step for me was to create a way that our group could offer objective and unbiased book reviews. The way to accomplish this was to create some type of book review standard where the reviewer can explain why a specific book received a certain star rating by looking at the same elements, while selecting the same set answers with a score attached, regardless whoever read and reviewed the book. I also wanted to insure that authors were held accountable for the types of books that they chose to publish from the moment that the reader considers purchasing their book.

I didn't want my book club members to give out a five star review to an author that had overpriced books, lots of grammatical errors, weak storylines, underdeveloped characters, favoritism for a specific author etc. I also wanted my members to be accountable for their reviews and how they scored them. At the end of the day, all reviews are reflective of our book club.

I do have to give credit to Martin Pratt of Urban Literary Reviews as well. He was a tremendous help with being my soundboard as I pulled the book review standards together. He also helped me to adapt the book review standards to use for non-fiction books as well.

The Steps to Creating Book Review Standards

Have you ever read reviews from different reviewers within the same group that you felt were just so much different from one another that you either stopped reading the reviews that were offered by that specific person or by the entire group because of the inconsistencies? Some may argue that reviews can vary because different people are reviewing books and to a certain extent this is true. But when we see reviews on opposite ends of the spectrum from the same group, it can be very confusing and looked at as unreliable reviews from the entire group.

Book review standards are basically essential elements that you feel should be present in all books that you'd like your reviewers to pay attention to while reviewing books for your group. Having these standards in place will help create consistency within the group so the reviews are not disproportionate. A simple discussion can easily help to create a standard for any group and should be talked about and put into place so that everyone is on the same page. When reviewers give a book five stars that has many grammatical errors; a synopsis that absolutely has nothing to do with the storyline; show obvious favoritism or even blatant disdain for an author and doesn't actually offer a review; that one unacceptable review can in fact hurt the group as a whole. It's true that reviews are mostly subjective but there are ways to give an objective review, while supporting your opinion by giving concrete examples of why the book was good or bad.

Anyone offering book reviews should display their book review standards on their website so authors and publishing companies can make an informed decision prior to submitting their books. If the author decides to send their book based on the standards that has been clearly displayed for all to see, they are ultimately saying that they are agreeable to your book review standards. By explaining your book review process on your website this can save the group time because it cuts down on answering the same questions multiple times and receiving the amount of undesirable books.

5 Essential Book Review Elements

As I've mentioned before, my book club decided to come up with five essential book review elements that we felt should be reflecting in every book we read as an avid reader. The five essential elements that we came up with includes:

- Book Presentation

- Book Price

- Storyline

- Character Development

- Editing

I believe that book club that decides to review books should be approached and written from an avid reader's prospective. What makes an avid reader pick up a book and consider purchasing it? What are the determining factors that would make one book more appealing over another if a reader only had enough money to purchase one book? If the reader hadn't been sent the book for review, would they have purchased it on their own based on the presentation and price? These are all great questions that I took into consideration when I decided to create book review standards because ultimately it's the reader that purchases the book.

Whether a reviewer realizes it or not, a book's presentation will affect how they critique books. Avid readers form an opinion about a book BEFORE they actually read the book. The title, cover, and synopsis are very crucial elements of a book because the book presentation is what ultimately peaks the reader's attention. The book's presentation should accurately represent the book's content, which is why this important element should be considered while reviewing books. When the book presentation and content is mismatched, this generally causes confusion and distracts the reviewer while reading because they will constantly stop to look at the cover and flip the book over to read the synopsis to make sure they are reading the same book. This misinformation will automatically cause the reviewer to question the storyline, dissect the characters, and pay closer attention to the editing because the book essentially doesn't make sense to them based on that first impression.

Avid readers are typically visual people. So if the book cover isn't pleasing to the eye; title doesn't jump off the page; the synopsis doesn't grab their attention; the book isn't going to sell regardless how good the reviews are because the book doesn't present well. So ultimately it doesn't matter how well written the book is. Keeping this in mind, I felt that a portion of a book review should be reflective on how the book presented itself because no matter what's in between the sheets avid readers always depend heavily on what they can readily see and read prior to purchasing a book which is the title, cover and synopsis.

Why choose five elements? Well simply because it was easier to adjust the book reviews to a five star review scale, which is pretty standard. It's fine for reviewers to make up their own rating scales but when you have a rating scale of 10, it's just way too much to keep up with and it really doesn't mean a lot to everyone that's used to a five star rating. Also, if the group wants to publish their reviews on other websites they will have to adjust their scores to a five star rating scale anyways. So why create a scale that's going to cause more work in the end?

How the Book Review Standard Works

Point Value System

Each element is worth up to an entire point. There are three standard responses that are offered for each element. The responses all correlate with a specific point that can be earned. The book will receive either 1 point, an half of a point or no points based on what the reviewer felt the book earned.

Constructive Feedback for Each Scored Element

After deciding which score to give each individual element the reviewer is asked to give an explanation on why the book received that particular score – good or bad.

Overall Review Based on the Scored Elements

The reviewer is asked to give a review in their own words that doesn't summarize the book or offer a second synopsis. The review should provide what the reviewer liked about the book, the elements that they felt needed to be improved and the overall thoughts of the book and if they would read the author again.

Optional Comments

The reviewer is also given the option to add an internal comment to whoever is in charge of collecting and posting the reviews or the author that's not published in the review.

Accumulative Score

The score from each of the five elements are added together to give an accumulative score (rating). This score is what we use as our rating for the book.

The Five Book Review Elements in Detail

Now that we've gone through how the review standard works, let's talk about the significance of each of the five elements.

Book Presentation

The first introduction to a book consists of the title, book cover and synopsis. If the title and cover are appealing, the reader will read the synopsis. If any of these three components doesn't present well, it can persuade the reader to not purchase the book. Here's a few tips for all three sections of the book presentation:

Title
The title should be catchy and pique the reader's attention.

Book Cover
The cover should give the reader what I call a "visual synopsis" of what the book is about.

Synopsis
If the title and book cover is appealing typically the reader will read the synopsis.

Book Price

Once the book presentation captures the reader's attention the only thing that can make or break a book sale is the book's price point. When looking at the price of the book you have to look at the page count, if the book is paperback or hard cover, and the genre in order to decide if the book is priced accordingly. A 200-400+ page all fiction and most non-fiction paperback books should be priced between $13-16. The genres that should be excluded are: reference (how to) books, school textbooks, technical books, picture (or illustrated) books etc. Do not take the sale price of traditional book or any price for electronic books into consideration because the price tends to vary. There are no standards in place for setting prices for electronic books. We have found it necessary to look at the price of books because of some publishing companies (generally vanity presses) or authors marking books up to ridiculous prices. Quite simply, a reader should never be asked to purchase a 200 page fiction trade paperback for $20.

Storyline

The storyline is one of the most important components of a book, next to the character development.

All books should offer a beginning, middle and ending, even if the book is a part of a sequel. It's important that the author give readers a complete storyline because the reader will be left with too many unanswered questions. This could cause the reader to not want to read another book by the author. Authors should be allowed to write whatever ending that they want to but the beginning and middle of the story must justify the ending.

You should think about the following questions in reference to the storyline: Was the storyline memorable? Did you feel that the author was able to support the ending of the story by building the story up? Did you feel like you receive a complete story? Did the author have too many holes in the story that should have been addressed? Would you recommend this book to others?

Character Development

The most memorable characters for readers are generally the ones that you never hear the author's voice come through. Characters are memorable because of their attitude, mannerisms, dialect and how they interact with other characters. The author's job is to make the reader feel some type of emotion for their characters - good or bad. The reader should be able to visualize the characters based on these characteristics, which will generally make them relatable and/or believable. If the author spends a lot of time describing what a character said or making the characters carry on meaningless dialog, this will cause the reader to not connect with the characters, despite the book itself offering a great storyline. Great character development to me is while reading a book the reader will get to a point where they know the characters so well that the author doesn't even have to mention who's speaking!

You should ask yourself the following questions in reference to the character development: Were the characters engaging? Were the characters believable and/or relatable? Where the supporting characters relevant to the storyline? Did the supporting characters overshadow the main characters?

Editing

Let me start out by saying that all books have a few missteps as far as editing is concern. I haven't read a perfectly edited book yet. When a book has multiple grammatically errors, words being used out of context, punctuation, sentence structure, wrong reference to time, place or historical periods/reference it's a challenge for avid readers to finish the book.

In reference to the book's editing you should ask the following questions: Did the book have editing issues took away from the storyline? Where there so many editing issues that it disrupted the storyline and made it a challenge to complete? Be honest so that the author is aware of the editing issues and can improve.

Putting it All Together

Now that we've identified the five important elements of a book review, explained how the book process works and discussed the five book review elements in detail, let's put all the pieces together and look at what the book review template look like.

I love digital templates and to be able to have access to everything from my tablet or smart phone. The book review form was created on a survey form via Respond-O-Matic. You can also use Google Documents or whatever you're familiar with. This will allow your reviewers to email you the form once they are ready to submit their review to you.

There are five sections in the book review form that will need to be completed:

- Reviewer and Book Information

- Book Review Elements Score System and Constructive Feedback Section

- Book Review Accumulative Score

- Overall Comments

- Personal Comments to the Author or Others (Optional)

Reviewer and Book Information Section

You should gather some information about the reviewer and the book on your review form.

- Reviewer's Name

- Email Address

- Name of Book and Author

- Page Count

- Was the book provided in paperback or hardcover? (if applicable)

- Suggested Retail Price (paperback or hardcover only - do not list sale or electronic book price)

- Genre

Book Review Element Score & Constructive Feedback Section

In the book review element score section you'll ask a specific question for each of the 5 elements. Each question is designed so that the reviewer will pay attention to the details within that specific element and ultimately provide an objective book review. It's important that the reviewers are able to give an explanation as to why they felt that the section deserved the score that they gave. For the person that receives the book reviews from the reviewers, they will be able to look over the score and the constructive feedback to make sure that they match. It's also important that the explanation makes sense and that the reviewer isn't scoring one way but their explanation is contradictory.

For each element there are three sections: a reviewer question; three standard answers/explanation with a specific point associated with each choice; along with a feedback comment box.

The following section includes the five elements exactly how they are written on the KC Girlfriends Book Club Book Review Standard Form:

Book Presentation

Book Presentation Question
Please think back to your first impression of the book. Would you have purchased the book on your own based

on how the book's title, cover, and synopsis are presented?

Book Presentation Score
1 pt Yes. Based on the book presentation, I would have purchase this book.

0.5 pt Maybe. There were a few issues that would make me second guess purchasing this book.

0 pt No. There were multiple issues with the book presentation that would make me not want to purchase this book.

Book Presentation Feedback
Please provide constructive feedback regarding the book's presentation.

Book Price
Book Price Question for the Reviewer
Based on the number of pages, the book type (hardback or paperback only), and genre: Is the price of the book comparable to other books in the same genre and size? *(You can only answer this question based on the retail price of a traditional book and not an electronic book due to there not being a standard retail price per size for ebooks.)*

Book Price Score
1 pt The book price is comparable to books in the same genre.

0.5 pt The book price is moderately overpriced compared to books in the same genre.

0 pt The book price is excessively overpriced compared to books in the same genre.

Book Price Feedback
Please provide constructive feedback regarding the book price.

Storyline

Storyline Question
What were your overall thoughts about the storyline? Did you feel that the author's story provided a beginning, middle, and an ending? Would you recommend this book to others based on the storyline?
Storyline Score
1 pt The storyline was memorable. I felt that I received a complete story. Yes, I would definitely recommend this book.

0.5 pt I felt that the storyline was average. I felt that I received a partial story. I might consider recommending this book.

0 pt The storyline was forgettable. I felt that the storyline did not offer a complete story. I would find it hard to recommend this book to others.

Storyline Feedback
Please provide constructive feedback regarding the storyline.

Character Development

Character Development Question
While reading the book, did you feel that the characters were engaging, believable and/or relatable? Did you feel that the supporting characters' presence were relevant to the storyline? (Consider all of the main characters and

any supporting characters that were significant to the storyline.)

Character Development Score
1 pt The main character(s) were engaging, believable and/or easy to relate to. The supporting characters were relative to the storyline.

0.5 pt The main character(s) were somewhat engaging, not fully developed, partially believable and/or somewhat relatable. The supporting characters were somewhat relevant to the storyline or were more believable and/or relatable than the main characters.

0 pt The main character(s) were NOT engaging, underdeveloped, nor believable and/or easy to relate to. The supporting characters were not relevant to the storyline and overall needed a lot of work.

Character Development Feedback
Please provide constructive feedback regarding the character development.

Editing

Editing Question
While reading the book, what were your thoughts about the book editing? (Please keep in mind that the majority of books (if not all) have a few editing errors. Editing errors can include grammar, word context, punctuation, sentence structure, wrong reference to time, place, or historical settings etc.

Editing Score
1 pt The book had none or very few noticeable errors.

0.5 pt The book had noticeable errors but DID NOT disrupt the storyline.

0 pt- The book had frequent errors that DID disrupt the storyline.

Editing Feedback
Please provide constructive feedback regarding the editing.

Book Review Accumulative Score

Total up the points from each section to figure out your review score. This score will represent your star rating for your review.

Note: I tend to drop the half point when placing receives on websites that doesn't allow half stars because the book did not technically earn the higher rating. I do state the exact score at the end of the written review when posting them on book store websites.

Score examples
     5 Stars = 5 Star Rating
4 & 4.5 Stars = 4 Star Rating
3 & 3.5 Stars = 3 Star Rating
2 & 2.5 Stars = 2 Star Rating
1 & 1.5 Stars = 1 Star Rating

Overall Comments

Please provide your overall thoughts/comments about this book. Please consider all of the elements that you've commented on above and do not include a synopsis or spoilers. (Your comments will be a part of the book review)

Note: It's really not necessary for the reviewer to summarize the book in order to offer comments about the book. Usually people just want to know what the reviewer's thoughts were about the book. The only time this should be done is if you're posting reviews on your website and maybe if you're posting it as a book review in a magazine. On other websites you should try to only post your overall thoughts and do not include any spoilers.

Comments for Person in Charge That Receive Reviews or Author (Internal)

Comments in this section will be shared with the author or the person receiving the review and will not be published as a part of the review. This is an optional field.

How to Write the Book Review

Generally when writing the review I will only post the reviewer's overall comments, which seems to work better than having to explain the entire process when offering the individual score and reasons in each section.

There are three parts that should be included in a book review:

1. First start off pointing out what you liked about the book.

2. Secondly, talk about what wasn't so great (or need improving) about the book in a constructive manner.

3. Give your overall thoughts about the book, which should include if you would recommend it to others and if you'd read another book by the author.

It's your choice if you'd like to forward the entire form to the author so they can see all of the comments and suggestions from each category. I would remove the reviewer's email address and last name first. It may be helpful to send this form to authors that received a low score. (I only send the form to authors that score lower than 3 stars.)

Questions You Should Ask Before Offering Book Reviews

Do you have enough members to create a book review team?

It's a good idea to have at least two or more book club members that will read more than one genre and that you feel they are able to offer an objective review.

Your reviewers should have enough time in their schedule to read books outside of the selected book of the month and return the reviews in a timely fashion.

You should strongly consider creating some type of book review standard so that everyone is on the same page, which should not be confused with controlling the reviewer's voice.

Which genres will you review?

You should be very specific on which genres your book club will accept so that authors do not waste their time sending you books that will not receive a fair review, if you're able to finish the book at all! You should state the genres that your book club will accept on your website.

It's essential that you only give books to reviewers in the genre that you know they will read.

How often will you accept and post reviews?

Determine how often you will accept book submissions by how much time your reviewers have to read.

If you see that reviewing books year around doesn't work for your group, consider accepting books during certain times of the year.

Where will you post reviews?

You should decide where you'll post your book reviews. Amazon would be the primary choice to post reviews but you should also consider other online book store websites, along with book lover friendly websites and social media websites.

Will you post bad reviews?

With all of the authors out there it's safe to say that you're going to receive a book or two that should not have ever seen the light of day! So with that being said, you should decide if you're going to post bad reviews or not.

If you do decide to post bad reviews (less than 3 stars), be sure the reviews are written in a respectful manner and give valid reasons why the book received such a low score. Remember, tasteless reviews reflect on your book club as a whole not necessarily just the individuals. Most people that read bad reviews don't remember the reviewer's name but the definitely will remember which book club they belong do.

How to Publicize That Your Book Club is Accepting Book Review Submissions

Let everyone know that your book club is ready to begin accepting book submission by advertising the information on your website or blog. Be sure to clearly state your book submission guidelines.

Post status updates on Facebook and Twitter on a regular basis to remind everyone that your book club is now offering book reviews. Be sure to use one of the book apps on Facebook and Twitter to post your reviews also! They will post automatically as a status update!

Chapter 7 Exercise

CREATING YOUR BOOK REVIEW STANDARDS

Now that you've learned how to create your own book review standards, jot down five important elements that you believe should be present in a book and which factors would determine the specific score.

Book Review Element #1

Book Review Element #2

Book Review Element #3

Book Review Element #4

Book Review Element #5

CHAPTER 7 NOTES

CHAPTER 7 NOTES

CHAPTER 8

COMMUNITY SERVICE AND FUNDRAISERS

Overview

Providing and/or participating in community service can be very rewarding and will allow your book club to give back to the community.

Holding fundraisers is a great way to fund community service projects and to cut the cost of your book club expenses. Some book clubs do very well with annual fundraisers and can count on people supporting them every year because they have built a great reputation with the community throughout the year, mostly by being active within their community.

Objectives

- Identify if community service and fundraising right for your book club

- When to think about when considering becoming a non-profit organization

- The difference between a nonprofit and not-for-profit organization

Is Participating in Community Service and Fundraising Right for Your Book Club?

Book clubs have the opportunity to make a difference in the lives of others by giving back to their community by volunteering or creating well needed services to a specific group in need, which can also enrich the lives of your book club members.

Fundraising is a way that your book clubs can actually cover costs for community service projects that you would like to either create or support. It can also help with covering costs for trips, author expenses, gifts or miscellaneous expenses. Some book clubs choose to do fundraisers instead of charging dues. It's a personal choice if your book club chooses to perform community service and fundraising. You should take into consideration what the makeup of your book club before you decide to perform community service and raising money.

Before you decide to participate in community service and fundraiser you should concentrate on getting your book club up and running. If you don't build your book club up first, you'll run the risk of overwhelming your members and yourself by introducing too much, too soon. While allowing your members to get acclimated to the book club, you should begin talking to them about your community service projects and fundraisers ideas so that they are aware what your long term goals are. You should give them a time frame of when you'd like to start on these projects. Allow your members to make suggestions on which types of community service projects and fundraiser they'd be interested in doing. This will help to create "buy in" by showing them that you want them to be a part of the planning of these projects and that you value their opinion.

You should answer these questions if you're thinking about doing community service and fundraisers:

- Why do you want to do community service?

- Who will benefit from the community service?

- What's the purpose for holding fundraisers?

- Are your book club members motivated enough to perform community service and/or to fundraise?

- Do you have buy-in from your book club members?

- Does your book club have time to do fundraising and/or community service?

- Will participation in community service projects and fundraising be consistent?

- Will the fundraising/community service be on going or at least annual?

Fundraiser Ideas

Fundraising can be a great way to defray the cost of being a part of a book club, along with raising money for other organizations or community service projects. It's really important that you consider doing any fundraising or community service projects that you have buy in from your book club members. Otherwise, your fundraising and community service efforts will not be successful.

Here's a few fundraising ideas that you may want to consider:

- Sell Greeting Cards/Calendars or other items.

- Coordinate a shopping trip to an outlet mall

- Conduct a raffle or silent auction

- Cook and deliver meals or desserts

- Sell advertisement space on your website

- Resale old books

- Hold an annual book club garage sale

- Create and sell a recipe book

Visit www.fundraiserinsight.org for more ideas.

Should Your Book Club Become a Nonprofit?

This is probably one of the most frequently asked questions by book clubs in reference to providing services to their community.

You should begin to consider becoming a nonprofit organization for the following reasons:

- If you plan on giving away scholarships.

- If you plan on offering a community service on a long term basis.

- If the community service projects requires funding and for you to ask solicit donations to maintain.

It would be wise to get involved in community service before you decide to become a nonprofit so that you have a good understanding how much work it is with coordinating, running and participating in community service projects. Having a great idea for community service projects and then carrying them out is two different things. It takes a lot of time, patience, effort, and resources to create and maintain a successful community service project.

There are certainly benefits that come with becoming a nonprofit organization. You can apply for tax exempt status. Donations that are given to your organization can be partially or completely claimed on the contributor's taxes. Nonprofit organizations generally receive great discounts or services. A lot of organizations will be willing to work with your group if you have established yourself as a nonprofit group.

You should do some extensive research on how to become a nonprofit organization and then make an informed decision about going through the steps to becoming a nonprofit. It's not an easy task and will take some time to get through all of the paperwork. You should definitely speak to an accountant and/or a lawyer that knows the proper procedure for creating a nonprofit entity to help you through the process. It's also a good idea to retain an accountant to help keep track of your finances and also help you file your taxes.

If you think that your book club is not quite ready to become a nonprofit group but would like to continue to provide services to your community, consider partnering with a nonprofit organization that is in the same field of interest as your project. This will help you receive some of the same perks without you having to go through the process of establishing yourself as a nonprofit entity right away.

What is the difference between a nonprofit and a not-for-profit organization?

The following is a very brief description to help you make the distinction between nonprofit and non-for-profit organization. You should do your research so that you fully understand all of the components of these two entities.

Nonprofit Entity
An organization that uses revenue/donations in order to help support a cause instead of distributing funds as a profit. A nonprofit organization has a board or controlling members. There may be paid staff members, employed non-paid volunteers and executives that serve on the board. Nonprofit organizations must have bylaws in place or in some cases submit paperwork to incorporate themselves in their respective state. Nonprofit organizations can also apply for tax exempt status.

Not-for-profit Entity
An organization that is permitted to generate revenue but can only keep the funds in order to help to preserve the organization, expansions or plans. Not-for-profits must have trustees, steering committee members, or board members in place.

Chapter 8 Exercise

CREATING COMMUNITY SERVICE & FUNDRAISING OPPORTUNITES

1. Create a list of community service projects that you would like for your book club to participate in.

2. Jot down ways that your book club can raise funds to help support your community service projects and/or your book club.

CHAPTER 8 NOTES

CHAPTER 8 NOTES

CHAPTER 9

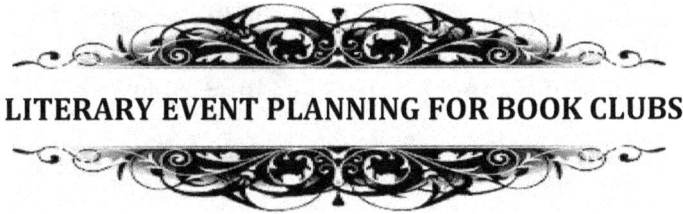

LITERARY EVENT PLANNING FOR BOOK CLUBS

Overview

Book clubs are known for creating their own literary events. I firmly believe that if book clubs do not see the type of events that they would want to attend in their area, they should be a part of the solution and create the type of event that they want to see. This is a great way to actually give back to your community and hopefully create an opportunity to network with other book clubs in your area. In this chapter we're going to go over planning different types of literary events for book clubs.

Objectives

- Learn how to prepare your book club for planning a literary event

- Identify the purpose for your literary event

- Identify the type of event to help support the specific purpose of your literary event

- Learn the different components for planning a literary event

- Discuss how to invite authors to a literary event

- Identify ways to promote the literary event

- Identify steps for hosting a literary event

- Discuss the post-event process

Host Book Signings Before You Start Planning Events

Planning a literary event is a lot of hard work and takes dedication. I always suggest that book clubs never begin planning an actual literary event until they have hosted a handful of book signings. Your book club should consider coordinating a literary event once your group is comfortable with hosting book signings. Here are a few reasons to start hosting book signings before taking on planning a literary event:

- Hosting book signings will help your book club to enhance your public presence within your community.

- Book signings are short and sweet and don't take much planning. Basically your book club would serve as the host. You can choose to supply a few door prizes and refreshments for the book signing.

- Book signings will allow your book club to network with local readers and book clubs, which is a great opportunity to gather contact information for newsletters so that you can notify book lovers about your upcoming literary events.

- Book signings are a perfect way to gather feedback from readers to see what type of literary event they would be interested in attending, and the authors that they would like to see. You should also ask them how they are enjoying the book signing they are currently attending.

- Authors will also take notice of your book club's willingness and ability to host book signings, which will help create a report with authors and also make it easy to secure them for future literary events.

Choosing the Type of Literary Event to Plan

Before you decide which type of literary event to plan you should know the difference between an event and a conference. Sometimes organizers use the word "conference" in the name of the event when it's not really a conference. So let's go over the definition of an event and a conference:

Events

Events take place with a common theme in mind and are usually held for approximately 2-5 hours. Events usually have at least one keynote speaker but can also have 2-3 additional guest speakers or guests as well. An event can be created for a handful of people up to hundreds – depending on the type of event you're planning.

Events can either be formal or informal and don't take as much time to coordinate or staff as a conference does. With that being said, you should at least give yourself 6 months or more to plan an event. If inviting authors to your event, you would want to begin sooner than 6 months so that you can begin to request their appearance before their schedule fills up.

Conference

The main purpose of a conference is to provide information or education on specific subjects, which are usually offered with specific meeting tracks for workshops, panel discussions, speakers or meetings etc. Conferences are generally held for a minimum of 5 hours but can last up to a week - give or take. Conferences have multiple featured guest speakers, which are usually experts or someone knowledgeable in the field of study that would be pertinent for the conference's purpose. If meals are not provided for the conference there are breaks for participants to purchase their own meals. Conferences are usually meant to have closer to 100 or more people in attendance.

Ideally, conferences should be planned at least 18-24 months in advance from the date of the initial conference. If the conference is going to be an annual event, planning for the following year will overlap with the current conference. Conferences are more formal than events because there are more components that make up a conference.

Defining Your Literary Event's Purpose

Once you've decided to coordinate a literary event it's really important that you figure out what the purpose of your literary event is before you begin planning. This will help you make the correct decisions in regards to coordinating the event. You may decide to change a few things along the way but you need to have some type of idea on what you want your event to look like, otherwise your event will not be organized or enjoyable to your guest.

You should ask yourself these questions in order to figure out the purpose of your event:

- Why do you want to create the event?

- Who is your target audience?

- How do you want your target audience to be impacted by attending your event?

Once you've answered these questions you need to figure out what type of event will be the best one to support your cause. The following are a few reasons for coordinating a literary event:

- Networking

- Introduction of a Product (i.e. book signing)

- Celebration

- Educational

- Entertainment

- Recognition

- Fundraisers

- Community Service

You may find yourself choosing more than one reason for coordinating a literary event from the list that's provided, which is fine. What's important is that you figure out the main purpose for the event in order to figure out the "Who, Why, Where, When and How" for the event.

When my book club decided to make our literary retreat a public event, we wanted to ensure that local book clubs, avid readers and authors would be able to create a network of support for one another. Authors and book clubs would learn about and support one another; avid readers could possibly find a great book club to join or be motivated to start their own book club while having great support as they are going through the process; everyone would leave the event inspired by our guest speakers, and more knowledgeable about the publishing industry and book clubs than when they arrived.

By creating a networking event, I knew that I wanted the event to be 3-4 hours and also include a meal. We reached out to three authors, who were more than happy to be our guest speakers and had lined up local authors and business owners as vendors. We actually lucked up on our venue. We were moved from a smaller hotel to a larger one by the facility once they heard exactly what we had planned. They agreed to give us a flat rate per plated meal with no taxes or gratuity added. We also did not have to pay a deposit or the room. We truly lucked up because none of this generally happens when you're dealing with hotels. This was the first time that I had coordinated an event like this before. It was nerve-wracking, exciting, intensive but in the end rewarding! The event was well attended and everyone had a great time.

Before You Begin Planning Your Event

Before you begin planning your event you should determine how much money and staff will be needed to adequately put on the event. It is extremely important that your book club members are 100% behind the event and are willing to assist. If the event that you're wanting to plan is something that you really want to do but do not have the support of your book club members it may be best to either wait until you gain their support, or coordinate the event outside the book club with other interested parties.

Fall Into Books Literary Conference is an event I felt would be best for me to coordinate outside of my book club because I knew my book club members were very busy with other activities. My book club members are very supportive of me and volunteer at the conference but the conference itself is not a KC Girlfriends Book Club event. Fall Into Books Literary Conference is a conference created through my business Literary-ly Speaking Events and Services. I knew that I wanted to step out and do something business-wise in literary event planning so the conference gave me this opportunity. Making this move has afforded me the opportunity to be hired as a literary event consultant and planner for other literary events.

Different Components for Planning an Event

Now that you've figured out the purpose for your event and what type of event you'd like to hold, let's look at the different components of planning your event. I'm going to basically give you a break down on what you should do in the event timeline section and then touch on a few pointers in each of the following components.

- Event Timeline

- Budget

- Venue

- Setting Ticket Prices

- Author Appearances Tips

- Vendors

- Onsite Book Stores/Carrying Books

- Advertising Your Event

- Managing Your Event (The day of)

Event Timeline

I think it's every important that you create a timeline for every component for your event. Your timeline should list the different tasks, any notes for your event, staff members and their assignments, and any deadlines. The timeline should begin from the time that you begin planning the event and throughout your event.

You should create your timeline while keeping the following in mind:

6 – 12 Months Ahead

(If you're planning a conference you should begin planning 12-24 months in advance)

- ***Purpose*** - Figure out the purpose for your event

- ***Planning Committee*** - Secure volunteers/Create committees

- ***Venue*** - Choose/Secure the Venue (Some venues require a deposit and some do not.

- **Registrants** – Set a goal on how many people you're projecting to attend. This will be important for setting your ticket price.

- **Budget** - Create a budget and lay out all of your expenses and income – decorations, venue, author expenses (if applicable), food, advertisement, printed materials (program/itinerary etc) and miscellaneous expenses. You should figure out how much money you have to contribute towards the event, how you're going to raise the funds and also come up with a ticket price, if your event will have a cover charge.

- **Food** - Choose a caterer or if you're working with a hotel obtain a menu so you can get a good idea of the costs. Don't forget to include the taxes and gratuity. If you're cooking your own food make sure you decide on a menu so that you can include the cost to over the food in your budget.

- **Collect Emails/Online Invitation** - Start collecting email addresses for updates/Create an online invite (once more details are known – you do not have to have all of the details into place to announce the event. If this is an event within 6 months of planning a "Save the Date" should be sent out at least a few months or more prior to the event. If you want people to attend from out of town, more time will be needed for people to plan ahead. Do not wait a few months prior to your event to get the word out.)

- **Hotel Reservations** - Reserve a block of rooms or create a list of nearby hotels if the event is not being held at a hotel.

- **Author Selection** – Determine how many featured authors you'd like to invite. Create a list and begin contacting them at least 6 months or more in advance.

- **Itinerary** – Create a preliminary itinerary so that you can begin to see how your event/conference will look and what you'll need.

- **Professional Assistance** – Determine if you'll need an event planner/consultant, decorator etc.

- **Promotion/Advertisement** – Determine how you're going to promote/advertise your event. (Should be online/offline promotion)

- **Sponsorship** – Identify sponsors that can help provide services and money
- **Create Letters of Agreement** – Create sponsorship letters, vendor contracts and letters of agreement for your featured authors.

- **Website** – Create a website or website page (if you don't already have a website) so that people can gather information about your event. Facebook invites don't count! If this will be an annual event you should determine if it's necessary to create a standalone website or add a new page to an existing website for the event.

- **Registration Fees/Collection** – Determine the cost for people to register once you've decided on a budget. Determine what method of payments you're willing to accept i.e. cash, check, credit cards and payments at the door. Determine how you're going to collect the fees i.e. PayPal, Eventbrite, or other online event registration methods, tickets in person only etc. Determine the deadline for advanced sales and when late registration will begin.

3 – 6 Months Ahead

- Letters of Agreement signed and returned- Have letters of agreement signed by authors (at least six months prior to your event)

- Gather bios for your featured guests (sooner if you're planning a conference or if you're wanting to place bios on your website about the featured authors)
- Send out 'Save the Date' emails/cards to announce your event (place information out earlier for conferences)

- Ensure that the featured authors and vendors are helping to promote your event and their appearance by placing the event information on their website. Be sure to tag authors in Facebook status updates and while Tweeting so that they will spread the word about the event.

- Begin purchasing decorations

- Begin creating a template for your program and place your featured authors' bios in the program. Announce ad placement for your program (if applicable).

- Circulate flyers about your event locally. Create a press release and submit to local media outlets. Place your event on online event calendars. Attend local and nearby events to hand out flyers. Email the flyer to friends, family, and coworkers so they can help spread the word. Create a list of where you placed flyers so that you can follow up and continue to supply more flyers if needed.

- Go back over your itinerary and begin adding speakers and other details regarding your event. Ask for a diagram of the space to help you visualize where everything should be placed. If there isn't one available be sure to go visit the site, take pictures and create your own diagram.

- Start thinking about the roles that your volunteers/committee members will play for the actual event.

- Create a logistical outline of all arrangements as they are being decided and confirmed.

- Be sure you're setting deadlines for tasks to be completed by the committees and receiving updates regularly.

- Send a list of the authors and requested books to the onsite bookstore for purchase at least 4 months prior to your event. This will give the bookstore enough time to find the books and let you know if they are having any difficulties locating a book

2 Months Ahead

- Committees should be meeting weekly. Entire group should be meeting at least twice per month, if not more, at this point.

- Request volunteers (if needed for the day of the event. This should be done well before now for conferences)

- Finalize your decorations and your facility arrangements.

- Begin purchasing flights and making transportation arrangements for featured authors (that you agreed to pay for).

- Double check with the bookstore to make sure the books have been ordered.

- Send out any updated details or a tentative itinerary to your featured guests and vendors so they have an idea of what to expect. Be sure that you stress that the itinerary is tentative and that you will email them a final itinerary a few days prior to the event.

- Continue promoting your event/check on flyers.

- Go visit the venue and make sure that everything looks good or request any repairs needed in the space. Go over food selections, centerpieces or any other decorations that will be provided by the facility.

- Begin placing more details into your program and placing purchased ads in the program.

- Export a registration report from your PayPal account or online registration service and create your registration list.

- Purchase your name badges, create your template, and begin entering your guests and staffs' names in the template.

- Remind registrants and anyone that needs to reserve a hotel room about the hotel registration deadline.

2 – 4 Weeks Ahead

- Begin writing introductions for your featured guests and also for your program.

- Create a production itinerary and schedule for internal use by your volunteers and committee.

- Begin putting together registration packages and book bags/stuffers for your event. Contact any sponsors for updates if you haven't received their items at least four weeks prior to your event.

- Make sure that all media outlets have received the information regarding your event. Work with media outlets to make sure that they promote your event.

- Contact your featured guests and vendors with any updates regarding the event and details that they need to know.

- Meet weekly with your committee to finalize any plans and program at this time. Go over the production schedule at the site and make any changes that are necessary.

- Be sure that you've received all of your PowerPoint presentations if applicable.

1 Week Ahead

- Print programs and itinerary.

- Hold a volunteer meeting.

- Hold a final production meeting with your committees.

- Print name badges and several copies of your registration list. Print out your welcome speech/key points, introduction etc.

- Make sure that you've uploaded everyone's presentations and ensure they are working correctly, along with any equipment being used.

- Confirm your numbers with the catering department at least 72 hours prior to your event.

Day of Event

- Arrive early

- Be sure you have your production schedule, itinerary/programs, registration lists, laptop to take credit card payments via PayPal if necessary, or take cash at the door if you're allowing onsite registration.

- Check the facility and make sure it is set up correctly.

- Set up your venue.

- Conduct sound and equipment checks.

- Set up registration early so that you're organized and can direct your vendors and registrants with ease.
- Follow your production schedule.

- Give yourself permission to have fun at your own event! You've earned it.

- Hand out a performance survey to attendees.

Post-Event

- Send personal thank you note or email to all of your featured guests, committee members, and volunteers.

- Finalize any outstanding balances from your event.

- Hold an event debriefing and talk about what worked and what didn't. Go over the attendee surveys.

Tips for Planning Your Event

Budget

When figuring out your budget, create two separate categories: 1.) Expenses and 2.) Income. Go back through the event timeline and choose which expenses you'll need to consider for your event. No need to create a budget template from scratch. Perform an internet search for 'event budget templates'. I've found that the templates that add your line items together and then compare your expenses and your income are the most helpful. You can stick with the categories provided or adjust, delete, or ignore them. Most of the templates will have exactly what you need and more, in order to create a budget.

If you're not sure what the exact expenses are for some of the items place an estimate for those items and then go back and readjust the number when you have the correct information. Most event budget templates are usually broken up into two pages or categories; one for estimates and the other for actual expenses.

Stick with your budget. If you need to adjust be sure to look at all of your line items and determine what you can afford to keep and let go of. Make a list of potential sponsors and begin contacting them before you adjust your budget. You should create a standard sponsorship letter that can be placed on your website or ready to email. Be sure to list that you're looking for sponsorship.

Venue

When choosing a venue be sure to READ THE ENTIRE CONTRACT BEFORE YOU SIGN IT! Most, if not all venues will have you sign an agreement with them in order to secure the space. Take another person with you or ask that the agreement is sent to you electronically where you can have others look at the agreement before returning it with a signature. No matter what, all agreements are negotiable BEFORE YOU SIGN IT! You can possibly have some minor details changed after signing the agreement depending on what you're asking for. But it's much better to have them adjusted in the contract before you sign them just to make sure that everyone's on the same page. **If you didn't receive it in writing it doesn't count!**

Hotels

I agree that hotels are so much nicer and accommodating than community centers, banquet halls, restaurants and schools, but nothing can replace the overall vision for your event, the outcome, and what people take home from it. Make sure it's absolutely necessary to hold your event in a hotel. Hotels have many hidden fees that you must take into consideration.

Meals – When looking at the menu, be sure to look at the bottom of the page to see what the gratuity and taxes percentages are. The prices listed on the menu do not include these extra costs. Your ticket prices should be reflective of these costs as well. Breakfast and lunch menu items are less expensive than dinner and finger foods. So if you can avoid dinners and finger foods this will definitely bring down your costs tremendously. Most hotels will not allow you to bring in your own foods.

Ask the hotel if you can sample dishes before you make your decision.

There's nothing wrong with having your members cook up some good food for your event if it is held at a different type of venue. Just make sure the members willing to cook can actually cook before they offer to make a dish. ☺

Cash Bars – You will usually have to pay for a bartender for your event. The charges can be per event and sometimes per hour.

Hotel Rooms – Check to see if you must guarantee a certain number of rooms be reserved for your event. If this is the case, be sure to stay below a number that you're confident you will be able to reserve. You can always go back and add more rooms to your block. Ask your event coordinator to email you regular updates for your room block. They will have the name of the people that reserved their rooms. This can also help you to reach out to everyone that hasn't reserved their rooms when you're nearing your deadline.

You do not have to hold an event at a hotel in order to block rooms at a special rate. Ask the venue that you're working with if they work with nearby hotels for special room rates. They should have a list of hotels ready for you. You will have to handle the details but it will give you a great start and you won't have to figure out which hotels are closest to your venue.

Be sure to do your homework before you decide to guarantee a room rate by doing an internet search on the hotel's website. If the hotel's website is not guaranteeing a cheaper rate than what they are advertising you should have your guest go directly to the website to secure their rooms instead of asking for a block. Or just hold enough rooms for the featured guests that you agreed to pay for their rooms.

Don't be afraid to hold your event at a venue that is not a hotel if you're expecting out of town guests. Most registrants will rent a car whether your event is located at a hotel, right next to the airport or, on a university campus, or in a downtown area. You should think of the most cost effective ways to save your registrants money without compromising your event's vision or purpose.

Other Venues

Make sure you consider other venues like community centers, libraries, restaurants, etc, especially if your event is only going to be 3-4 hours. These venues can be very low or at no cost to you.

Please note that you may have to do more work as far as setting up the venue on your own or paying for these services.

Tables and linens may be an added service that you'll need to pay for.

Make sure that you include enough time to set up and breakdown your event.

You may need more volunteers in order to help with your event in these types of venues.

The times that you can hold your event may be limited.

These events may charge by the hour or only limit you to a certain amount of hours for your event. Be sure you check with the event coordinators for all the details.

If you decide to use a caterer make sure that you ask the venue if the caterer has to be on their list of caterers. Also ask if the caterer has to sign a separate contract or if you or the caterers have to carry any incidental insurance and the amounts. (Most venue websites will give you these details.)

Setting Ticket Prices

When setting your ticket price you first need to settle on a realistic number of people that you expect to register for your event. You need to list all of your budget expenses that are not being covered by sponsors or your book club.

Expenses such as food, printed program, book bags, t-shirts etc. should be listed as an individual line item per person. Expenses such as feature author travel, food, and lodging expenses, venue room expenses, decorations, entertainment etc. should be divided among the set registration goal.

Example (See figure 1) – You have 100 people estimated to attend your event. Below, I've included a breakdown of what your expenses will look like if you have no sponsors or revenue to help cover expenses. You can see how important it is to either have sponsors or to cover some of the expenses for your event. My book club will generally cover all of the expenses for one featured author for our literary retreat. The other two featured authors are local so we only have to cover their meal. These expenses are covered with the dues we've paid over the past year. Covering author expenses helps decrease the ticket price for our registrants. We also do not have to worry about how many people register in order to pay for these expenses.

Other ways to cover author travel and lodging expenses would be to partner with other book clubs, find a sponsor, or only reach out to local or nearby authors. You can also have fundraisers throughout the year or raise your dues. Selling vendor tables or ad space in your programs is also an effective way to raise funds.

You can also see how easy some items can be omitted or can actually become revenue for your event like, book bags and t-shirts. By allowing your registrants to preorder these items and adding a few extra dollars this can create a source of revenue. Pre-ordering these items will also allow you to order the specific amount needed so you're not stuck with left over items that you may not be able to use after your event. Total ticket cost is configured with 100 people estimated in attendance

Figure 1 How to Calculate Ticket Prices

Figure 1

Expense	Cost	Per Person
Food	$30	$30
Venue	$500	$5
Printed Programs	$400 for 100	$4
Book Bags	$5	$5
T-shirts	$600 for 100	$6
Author Expenses	Lodging: $200 – 2(1) night stay	$2
(2 authors)	Travel: $600 - 2 airline ticket	$6
	Food: $60 – 2 authors' meals	$.60
Decorations	$500	$5
Entertainment	$500	$5
Misc. Expenses	$4.40 (can be any small and reasonable amt)	$4.40
	Cost Per Person	$73.00
	PayPal Fees Per Person	$2.00 est.
	Total Cost Per Person	$75.00

Letter of Agreements

Letters of Agreement are very important to have signed by your featured authors anytime that you coordinate an event. A letter of agreement is a contract between the author and yourself that states what services each party will provide in order to secure the author's appearance. This may seem formal but it's very necessary so that there is no miscommunication on what is to take place. If you do not have a letter of agreement in place, everything you agree to is basically up for interpretation. Letters of agreement do not have to be elaborate but should include the following:

- State the particulars about your event (Who, When, Where)

- State all of the expenses that your group will pay for.

- State what services the author is expected to perform.

- State who will handle the author's book sales at your event.

- State if either party can void the contract. If so, what are the circumstances?

- State who is responsible for paying the expenses if the author doesn't appear.

Make sure you act professional from the moment that you contact an author to request an appearance to the time they return home and thereafter. You're building a relationship with the author so how you treat them will determine if they will return for future events and also what they will share with other authors.

Make sure that the author is promoting their appearance for your event on their website and also ask them to share the information via their Social Media outlets.

Vendors

If you decide to allow vendors to participate in your event you should determine if you will charge for the space.

- Decide how much the table will cost and what will be included with the space. You should base the price of the table on how much the registrants must pay to attend and also your expenses.

- Have a letter of agreement in place so that all of the terms are spelled out.

Onsite Book Stores/Carrying Books

If you're hosting an author who is published through a traditional publishing house, you'll either need to have an onsite book store at your event to sell their books or you can purchase books directly from the publishing house at a discount. Unless you're purchasing books for everyone that registers for your event it may be best to contact a book store at least six months in advance to request their services.

Advertising Your Event

It's important that you begin advertising your event as soon as possible. Advertising your event is most effective if you have multiple people helping to spread the word. Events must be promoted online and offline. The majority of people may get online for various reasons but most of them will not seek out your website to find out if your book club is hosting an even. Think of the various places that readers may frequent and begin spreading the word. Here are a few ideas to help create a buzz about your event online and offline.

Offline

- Attend as many community events as possible, especially if they have vendor tables available.

- Place flyers in different locations: libraries (if the event is free), hair salons, college and university campuses, grocery stores, work places (work newsletters), email flyers to friends, family and coworkers.

- Make sure that all of your book club members are talking about the event online and off line. You should also consider having each member sell a certain amount of tickets as well. Remember – it's the entire group's event, not just your event. Everyone should be willing to help make the event as successful as possible. As long as you give your members enough time to sell tickets there should not be a problem with them helping to promote and sell tickets.

Online

- Website - Create a website so that people are able to learn all of the details about your event. This will also help cut down on multiple inquiries concerning information that should be readily available on a website.

- Facebook Event - Create an event on Facebook. Send out reminders periodically about your event and encourage people to register.

- Twitter - Send out information on Twitter. Twitter only works if you use it effectively, which means that you have to use Twitter regularly in order to see the benefit.

- Social Event Websites – Do a web search for online social event sites, especially ones that target your area. You should also place your event on Eventful.com, which will send your event information to countless event calendars that are in your area and nearby.

- If you do not have time to get on Facebook or Twitter on a regular basis sign up for Hootsuite or some other type of social media account that will allow you to send out scheduled Facebook status updates or Tweets. Most of these social media accounts are free.

Managing Your Event (The day of)

Planning your event is one thing but managing your event is an entirely different animal! Here are a few tips on getting through your event:

- Production Meeting - Make sure you hold a production meeting a day or two before your event with your volunteers and book club members. (You can also choose to hold a volunteer meeting separately.) This is when you'll actually walk through the entire program from beginning to end to explain exactly what should take place, when it should take place, who is responsible, etc. You should work with the venue and see if you can walk through the space with your staff and the hotel staff, if possible.

- Take your itinerary and include the details about your event (this itinerary shouldn't be given out to your attendees). You should also include who is responsible for which author, the author's flight itinerary, and hotel reservation information. Also include the times that your guest speakers are to speak, who is introducing the speaker, etc.

- Make sure you list where everyone is supposed to be at all times so that if anyone needs help they know where to look. Include everyone's cell numbers. Texting is a great thing when you can't be everywhere at the same time.

- Make sure you have people on your staff that can make minor decisions on your behalf. You should also have a "go to" person as well. You'll be running in many directions and will more than likely be presenting or speaking a lot during your event. (Minor decisions shouldn't cost you money or need your signature. If that's the case you should be contacted when you're available to make those decisions before anything is done.).

- Make sure you're well rested before your event. (I know this is a hard one but it's important that you're well rested, eating right and full of energy. Your day will start early and end late. I struggle with this one but the best way to help this along is to stick with your deadlines, make sure everything is completed on time and don't have too many tasks to finish at the very end.)

- Make sure you print out several production schedules and place them in folders so that you know exactly what they are when you see one. Also, set a production folder with all of your introductions and anything that needs to be announced, along with a regular itinerary at the podium so that you always have one handy.

- When creating your souvenir program DO NOT include the itinerary in the program. Instead, print the itinerary separately. This will save money. Usually people will pick up an extra program because they want to replace the itinerary that they lost. This will allow you to print a few copies of the program outside of the number you'll need and allow you to print as many itineraries as you'd like. Although colored programs and itineraries are nice, it is not necessary. If you can afford to pay for color then do so, if not, don't sweat it. Just make sure the program looks great and the printing is of good quality.

- Make sure you sit out in the audience whenever possible throughout your event so you can see what your attendees see. I always take notes during my events so that I'm always improving. I'm an avid reader first and have attended many different literary events. I want to see my events from the author's and book store's eyes as well. Make sure you're checking on your guests. You should also have someone on hand to help you with hospitality to make sure everyone is getting what they need, when they need it.

- Be flexible and know that there is no such thing as a "perfect" event. Situations come up all the time. Don't stress out; fix the problem! Unless you have a situation that you must announce to your attendees, never let them see you sweat. Take everything in stride and move forward with your itinerary. You have all the time in the world after the fact to figure out what happened so you can improve the next time. Sometimes, some of the best laid out plans don't work when you execute them. That's life. (This is also why you need to make sure you have strong and low stress people assisting you. Your staff should be able to work well under pressure. If not, you'll spend more time taking care of them, as opposed to addressing the problem!)

- Most of all – make sure you take the time to enjoy yourself at your event. I can say that I always do this and it's great to be able to sit back and be able to enjoy your hard work. Be proud of yourself!

No exercise for this chapter! Make a template of the timeline and start planning a great literary event whenever you're ready! ☺

CHAPTER 9 NOTES

CHAPTER 9 NOTES

CHAPTER 10

STEPS TO CREATING A TEEN BOOK CLUB

Overview

Encouraging teens to read for enjoyment can sometimes be a hard task. Choosing the correct types of books can pique the interest of any young reader, along with creating a positive environment for the youth to discuss social issues that impact their everyday lives. Offering a community based book club can also be an asset to the community.

Although this chapter will be talking specifically on how to create a teen book club - specifically kids in high school, you can adjust the information offered in this chapter to any age group of readers.

Objectives

- Discuss the benefits of starting a teen book club

- Identify community resources

- How to select appropriate books and different purchase options

- Discuss appropriate bylaws
- How to facilitate a meet and greet

- How to facilitate an effective book club meeting

Benefits of Starting a Teen Book Club

Positive Environment & Social Interaction

Book clubs can provide a positive environment for young readers, which can help to support their love of reading. There are many teens that love to read but most times they have no one to really discuss books with, which sometimes can cause them to not read as much as they should. Teens need a variety of ways to interact with others in a social setting outside of their normal routines. Discussing books that teens can relate to not only helps to sharpen their reading and comprehension skills but also creates a support system for teens. Discussing books can also help others to be more accepting of other people's opinion and to learn how to communicate more effectively. Creating a teen book club can also help to teach teens how to become more active in their own communities, along with exposing them to different aspects of the literary industry.

Platform to Discuss Social Issues

One of the greatest benefits for creating a teen book club is that it will create a platform for teens to discuss social issues that impact their daily lives. This is done by choosing appropriate aged books that are relatable. Discussing books in a warm atmosphere can evoke a very honest dialog among teens. It's important that the book discussion allows them to talk about how the books made them feel and not just about the story. As the teens participate in more meetings they may start to feel comfortable sharing examples from their personal lives, which should be done without judgment from other members. If you are a part of a book club, you've probably already experienced these kinds of conversations and know how book discussions can compel you to share personal experiences.

Introduction of Different Genres

By creating a teen book club you also have the opportunity to expose them to different genres. Remember, book clubs are about exposing yourself to new books, not just about reading what's familiar. Teens should be reading fiction and non-fiction books. Start out with genres that you feel will grab their attention first. Once you've established the book club begin choosing books in different genres to help teens expand their knowledge. Classic books are also an option but I definitely would not start out reading a lot of them because it sometimes symbolize what teens find wrong with reading. Make sure all of the book selections are appropriate for the age group that represents the book club.

Opportunity to Connect with Authors

Most teens have never had the opportunity to meet an author. Although it's not possible to have each author personally sit down with your group, you can however use video conferencing or conference calls to have the majority of authors participate. Connecting young readers to the authors can help to answer questions that they may have about the book and can also give them an insider's view on how books are written. You may also have potential writers in your bunch, which can also help to encourage them to pursue their passion of writing or anything else they may want to do in life. Teens should also attend book signings and other literary events, if possible, to help encourage them to continue to read.

Community Resources

Identifying community resources is essential for recruiting and with providing assistance with securing a facility to hold meetings or to provide books (if needed). Most organizations will be more than willing to help or may have other resources available. We're going to discuss some great resources below.

School Libraries

School librarians are probably the most valuable resource you will have in respect to recruiting and providing resources for your teen book club. School libraries can connect you to teens and can also help provide books or book resources if needed.

Each school district provides contact information for all schools, including the person in charge of the library and also their email address. Collect all of the contact information that you need and place it in a spreadsheet to help keep track of the information that you've gathered.

If you live in an area that has neighboring states like in the Kansas City Metropolitan area, it'll be important to decide which areas of the city you will concentrate on and then contact those librarians first. You can always expand out of to other areas if you want to recruit more readers.

Because you want to work with children, it's really important that your book club have a website so that you are able to refer the librarians just to help confirm the legitimacy of your book club.

Emailing librarians first will help save time and money. Using email can also help you keep track of your correspondence with the librarians. You can also choose to follow up with sending a letter with a flyer attached is also a great idea if you haven't received a response within 7-10 days. Placing phone calls is also an option as well.

Public Library Branches

Your local public library systems are wonderful resources because they can provide meeting space and can also help provide your group's book of the month selections. Another benefit of holding your book club meetings at a library branch is that your meeting information will be listed on their website and newsletters, which can help with recruiting members. If you choose to hold your book club meetings elsewhere, libraries generally will allow you to hang flyers on their bulletin boards to help with recruitment.

Local Book Clubs

Local book clubs can be very resourceful by helping to spread the word about your new teen book club. They may also have children that could be interested in joining your book club. You should also consider asking local book clubs to partner with you to help start your teen book club as well. Some book clubs may also hold book drives or may be interested in sponsoring portions of your book club by either purchasing books or donating money.

Book Stores

You should reach out to local book stores to inquire about discounted bulk book purchases for you books. Book stores are definitely book club friendly so you should seriously consider using space in a book store to hold your monthly meetings.

Organizations

Organizations such as: YMCA, Boys & Girls Club, Churches, Greek Organizations etc. can be wonderful resources for your book club, especially if you have any affiliation with any of them.

Social Event Calendars/Websites

If your city has a social event calendar or website that allows you to post information be sure to utilize these resources so that you can make the public aware of your book club. It is also a great idea to think about creating your own website for your book club as well. You can place meta-tags in your website, which will make it easy for anyone searching for a teen book club in your area. (Meta-tags are key words that you place in your website to help people search for you based on words that describe what they are looking for i.e. Kansas City teen book clubs, teen book clubs in Kansas City area, teen book clubs in Missouri etc.)

Be sure to include the following information in your email when contacting community resources:

- Explain who you are and your book club affiliation

- The purpose of your email

- What services you're asking them to provide

- What you hope to accomplish

- When you're expecting to start the book club

- Attach a flyer that can be printed and placed in the common area of the school with the essential information needed.

Selecting Appropriate Books

It's crucial that you choose the appropriate book selections for your teen book club. Begin choosing books that you feel that teens will be able to relate to first. Books that talk about social issues will help peak their interest and keep them reading. Most teens will read books by most Young Adult authors as long as it captures their attention. To begin searching for books try to look up books that are award winning. This will at least ensure that you have quality books. Once you find a few books that are to you liking, you should go on any online book store website and find some of the award winning books that you research and you should begin to see books that are similar to the book that you originally searched for. This will help you to find books that may be good for your group. Sometimes it's hard to find the type of books that you want for your group, especially books for African American teens, but they are out there (See Resource chapter for suggestions). Keep in mind, if you're starting a group for a specific race, teens generally do read books across the board and do not see color when choosing books. It's great to always try to introduce books written by authors that are of the same race, which I do encourage but do not limit the group to just one type of author if your group enjoys books by all authors. Each book club is different. Do what's best for your group to get the best outcome.

Make sure that your book selections are age appropriate. You should be able to find an age range on all Young Adult books. This is also why you should consider separating or choosing High School and Middle School teens. Most books are not meant for middle school aged children to read. If you choose to have both age ranges to participate in the same group, this will limit your choices. Some topics that may be discussed in books may not be quite appropriate for younger teens. You do not want to introduce certain subjects to children that may not have been discussed with their parents first. This is also why you should always provide the book cover and the book description to the teen's parents so that they are aware what you intend to read with them. This will give the parent a chance to read the book and discuss certain issues that are presented in the book before the child has a chance to read it. It's really important that you make sure that you have the parents buy in when dealing with teens. This is also a great opportunity to get the parents to participate in meetings as well.

Book Purchasing Options

Most teens, especially high school aged teens, have jobs so purchasing books aren't always an issue. If you are dealing with a group that has barriers with purchasing books, there are a few options that you may have in order to cut costs.

Discounted Books

Try to purchase books at a discount from your local book store or online. Most local bookstores will offer discounts and some may decided to donate a certain number of books from time to time to help your group out. Online book stores are great because they usually offer various options to purchase books. Sometimes books can be as cheap as $.01. You should also visit author and publishing house websites to see if they offer book club discounts. Some publishing houses also have community programs that donate books for events and worthy causes.

Electronic Readers

Although the majority of avid readers still love hard or soft cover books, electronic readers are definitely a great alternative and should be considered to decrease the cost of books. The prices of electronic readers are decreasing dramatically and are becoming very affordable. Most teens own smart phones nowadays and have the capability of downloading the Kindle and/or Nook app onto their phone, which is free. Downloading these electronic readers on a laptop or desktop computer is also an option as well. You should also check with your local library system to see if they have your books available for download.

Book Buddy Share Program

Ideally, you'd like for everyone to purchase the selected book each month but sometimes families may be unable to afford books from time to time. If you find that your teens are struggling with purchasing books every month you should consider instilling a book buddy share program. This doesn't have to be done with everyone but maybe the ones that are having problems affording books every month. Basically two members would be responsible for paying for a book every other month and each member would have two weeks to read the book selection. This will help share the cost of the books and hopefully decrease the burden of purchasing a book every month. This can also be done with electronic readers as well by having the two members sign up on the same type of device, which would enable them to share the book.

Donations

You can also seek out organizations that would be willing to purchase books for your group.

Teen Book Club Bylaws

Teen book club bylaws are not too much different than a regular book club. Essentially you want to include all of the essential information that involves your book clubs. While creating your teen book club bylaws make sure to include the following information. You may replace or incorporate these components for your bylaws, which were discussed in Chapter 4:

- Include a strong mission and/or purchase statement.

- Logistical information for your meetings: date, place and time
- Include a book order deadline date. This will insure that all members purchase and receive their books on time. You should also choose 3-4 books in advance so that books can be purchased at one time to save on shipping cost.

- Include the book club's website information where they can find all of the necessary information, along with contact information where they can reach you.

- Include all of the required group activity information

- Include a code of conduct.

- Include all expenses to be paid for by members.

- Include dues

The Two Cents Rule

"You must read the book selection and come to the meeting prepared to give the group your two cents or you must pay two cents per page that you failed to read and didn't come prepared to discuss."

The two cents rule is something that I incorporated into my teen book club from the beginning in order to make sure that the members understood what was expected of them like reading the selected books on time and participating in the discussions. Book clubs will only work if the members read the book selections, show up for meetings and are ready to discuss the book. Without these things in place there is no book club.

It's better to have a group of avid readers as members of a book club but you may have some young people that are trying to establish better reading habits. Regardless how often the members read, the bottom line is that being a part of a book club is no different from any other type of extracurricular activity. It takes commitment and a lot of effort on their part to be a productive member of any group; book clubs are no different.

Teen Book Club Meet & Greet

Before you begin holding book club meetings it's really important that you hold a meet and greet with the potential book club members and their parents. Holding a meet and greet gives everyone the opportunity to get acquainted with one another and also ask questions about the book club. It's really important that you have to have a parent or guardian present at the meeting. Try to set up a time that's convenient for most. If there other people interested in the book cub you can decide to hold a conference call for a group of people at one time or call everyone individually.

Here are a few tips to help you with your meet and greet:

Create a welcome folder that includes the following:

- Itinerary

- Bylaws

- Agreement

- Parent permission slip

- Parent/Member contact form

- At least 3-4 book selections with the book description

Hold the meet & greet at the facility where you plan to hold your regular book club meetings if possible.

Play an ice breaker game that allows the guests (including parents) to get to know everyone in the room.

Explain the book club and what your plans are for the book club.

Explain the bylaws and have the teens sign an agreement that they understand and are agreeable to the terms of the bylaws.

Go over the book selections. You should have at least 3-4 books selected, along with the book description, book cover and purchasing information available.

Have parents sign a form giving permission for their child to participate in the book club. You should include a description of the type of subject matters that may appear in the book selections and what the parent's responsibilities are and how to proceed if there are concerns with any books that will be read by the group. You also need the parent's contact information and should get permission to transport their child, especially if your group plans on taking trips somewhere.

How to Facilitate an Effective Teen Book Club Meeting

Create Engaging Book Discussion Questions

It's really important that you create an atmosphere that's fun and engaging! In order to have your members participate in an effective book discussion you really have to be a great facilitator. If there aren't any book discussion questions available at the back of the book, be sure to write down a few thoughts that you had while reading the book and develop questions based on your thoughts. Many times some of your members may have thought of the same questions.

Play Icebreaker Games

Playing ice breaker games can help your members to get better acquainted with one another. A simple internet search can result in hundreds of games that you can adapt to your book club. You can also create crossword or word search puzzles and give out small prizes as well.

Create a Mobile Text Club

Most all teens have a mobile phone and definitely text! Creating a mobile text club can help you to send out one message to everyone, instead of having to call everyone one at a time. Parents can also sign up as well. Mobile text clubs can also help your group keep up on their reading by creating a book text trivia game. If your members use Twitter you can send the question out and create a hashtag so that it's easy for them to locate the question. Have them to send their answers in a direct message. (This can also be adapted for Facebook)

Book Text Trivia Game Instructions

1. Give the group one week to obtain the book.

2. Divide the chapters or page count into three parts and then choose a question from one of the chapters per predetermined section

   Example: Your selected book has 21 chapters. The first question will come from chapters 1-7. The second question will come from chapters 8-14. The Third question will come from chapters 15-21. Generally book clubs meet on a monthly basis so there should only be 3 questions per month, unless your members want to do more questions.

3. Text the questions at different times of the day so that everyone has an opportunity to respond to at least one question.

4. Whoever responses back first with the correct answer win a small prize, which should be given at the next meeting. In order to keep the game going, create a grand prize drawing to be given away once a year. The winner of the week will have their name placed in the grand prize drawing twice. Anyone that responds with the correct answer in a certain amount of time (limit the response time to 2-3 hours) will have their name placed in the grand prize drawing once.

Allow the Teens to Discuss without too Many Adult Interjections

As the adult, you want to step back and allow the teens to really discuss the book between them. Once the discussion question has been answered you should then give your prospective. Sometimes adults can inadvertently interject their opinions, which can come across as being judgmental. This can cause some teens to not feel comfortable sharing. Restate some of the points that were made during the teen's discussion to pose a question to the group and to keep the conversation going.

Make Sure Everyone Participates

Going around the room will insure that everyone has a chance to participate if the members aren't doing so on their own. Making sure that all members participate in the discussion will also assist you in seeing who's reading the books. If it's too difficult or lengthy to go around the room to have members answer each question you can always have a certain amount of members respond but just make sure that you include the members that weren't able to answer in the next discussion question. You may also want to think about limited the amount of time that each member has to answer a question by setting a timer for 2 or 3 minutes. Whoever is in possession of the timer is the only one that can speak. This will allow everyone to not only speak but to also be heard.

Invite Authors to Participate In Book Club Meetings

Consider having authors discuss their book with your group. Most teens have never met an author before, let alone discussed a book with one before. Having authors participate during book club meetings can be made easy by having the author join your book club meeting via video or conference calls. Discussing books with authors can bring an entirely different prospective when reading a book. It also allow the members to ask the author questions that the book that they may want clarification about or about their writing career.

Connecting with authors can be as easy as just sending them an email request. You want to make sure you send your request as soon as possible in order to secure their appearance. You should also make it a point to see if the author will be appearing in your area around the time of your meeting and either invite the author to sit down with your group or meet them at their book signing. Some authors may not have a lot of time or an extra day to meet with your group at a separate location but you may be able to meet with the author before or right after their book signing at the book store if time permits. This is also why you want to reach out to the author as soon as possible. They may be able to rearrange a few things if given proper notice.

Participate in Joint Teen Book Club Meetings

Again, because of today's technology, it's really easy to connect with other book clubs from around the country. You should look for local teen book clubs that you can possible reach out to first. Discussing books together can be really fun with other groups and it also helps to connect with others for resources and support. Meetings can be conducted at the same location, video conferencing or conference calls.

Other Book Club Tips:

Avoid Busy School Schedules

Be sure you're checking with the school district's calendar for holidays and tests that are coming up. You may want to either eliminate that meeting altogether or choose an alternative date. Finals and standardized tests can be stressful and should be the focus during that time. In order to be consistent you still meet but choose to do a social activity instead of reading a book. Some times readers will surprise you and want to read despite what's going on. Assess to see where your readers are at and then make a decision.

Think Ahead! Weatherproof Your Meetings

Unfortunately, we never have control over the weather. With that being said, it's really important that you have an alternative in place for your book club meeting if the weather is a factor. A conference call meeting is a great alternative to meeting in person. This will not only help keep everyone safe but keep your meetings consistent. Again, if all of your members are connected with social media you should consider meeting online to discuss the book on Twitter or in a Facebook group.

Start Your Teen Book Club in the Summer

Consider holding your teen meet & greet in late spring and begin your regular book club meetings at the beginning of summer.

Teen book clubs can begin anytime but there are great advantages for beginning your book club outside of school months. If you begin the book club during the time summer the teens will have more time to read, which will give them time to become an avid book reader! Avid readers are more consistent with reading and will make the time in their schedule during school time.

Chapter 10 Exercise

ORGANIZING YOUR TEEN BOOK CLUB

This exercise is to help you to get organized while planning to start your teen book club.

1. Gather the names of a few organizations that you'd like to approach about starting your teen book club.

2. Do you want to start a book club within an organization or do you want them to help assist you with certain aspects of the book club?

3. Create a list of people/organizations that can help you recruit members.

4. Create a reasonable timeline to have your teen book club up and running.

CHAPTER 10 NOTES

CHAPTER 10 NOTES

CHAPTER 11

STEPS TO REVITALIZING YOUR BOOK CLUB

Overview

Sometimes book clubs go through a phase where the glue that once held the book club together begins to weaken, which can threaten the existence of the book club. So what now? Do you revitalize or dissolve your book club altogether? Is a bad book club member causing others to suffer or is the entire foundation of your book club need to be restructured and strengthened? We'll answer these questions plus more in this chapter.

Objectives

- How to recognize when your book club is in trouble

- Identify if your book club can be repaired or should be dissolved

- Dismissing members with love

Is Your Book Club in Trouble?

Maintaining a book club can be just as hard as creating one. Nothing is written in stone and just like people can change so can the dynamic of your book club. Overtime you can learn what works for your book club but you should always be willing to adjust in order for your book club to stay active.

We're going to discuss some common reasons why book clubs tend to get into trouble and a few tips on how to correct the issues:

Failure to Support the Mission Statement

Most times, book clubs tend to lose their way because decisions are being made that do not encompass the mission statement. Remember your mission statement is what will help you make decisions to help support your book club's purpose for existing. Sometimes your mission statement may need to be adjusted because your book club decides to include or omit certain ideas as your group grows. This is normal. You should go back and adjust your mission statement to fit your group and move forward if this is the case.

You should ask yourself the following questions:

1. Is your book club living up to its mission statement? Why or why not?

2. Do you need to be more consistent with implementing your mission statement or need to adjust your mission statement altogether?

Book Club Meeting Turns into a Social Meeting

One of the biggest issues that some book clubs have is really with the members not reading the book selections but still showing up to meetings. You may need to remind your member from time to time that your group is a book club first and a social club last. It's not acceptable to show up at book club meetings without being prepared to discuss the book. If you allow this behavior to continue other book club members may think its okay to show up without reading the book as well and then the next thing you know, none of your members are prepared to discuss the book.

Not reading the book selections can be very embarrassing if you decide to have an author participate in a book discussion as well. It's not acceptable to have an author take time out of their schedule with the intentions of discussing their book with a book club that's not prepared to do so.

Discord Between Members

Sometimes book club members that are having issues with one another can affect the entire group. If there are issues between two members speak to both parties and make sure they are aware how they are affecting the group. Ask them to address their differences outside of the book club meeting and not get others involved with their issues. Stay neutral between the two members and try not to take sides. If either person continues to address their issues during book club gatherings it may be necessary to ask one or both members to leave the book club. Experiencing discord between members can make a very uncomfortable environment and also cause your loyal members not want to be a part of the group. Do what's right and save your group.

Inconsistent Meeting Times

It's really important that your book club meetings do not change from month to month. Most book club members will get confused and more than likely miss meetings out of sheer confusion. Book club facilitators should help to facilitate meetings but should not be able to change the time or date of the meetings. Unless your book club meeting falls on a holiday do not change your book club meeting dates or times.

Bad Book Selections

Consistently choosing bad book selections or even choosing the same authors all the time can make your book discussions dull. Make sure you pay attention to the types of books that your book club tends to like and dislike. I have learned through the years exactly which genres do not work for my book club, which ones they love and the few genres that they are willing to at least try out. Individually, some of my book club members do read all genres but as a group it just doesn't work for us.

Choosing several of one particular author's work (unless this is why you created your book club...which shouldn't really happen) to read within a year is always a bad idea. One of the joys of being in a book club is to actually challenge yourself to read authors that you probably would not have read on your own. You can always read other books by your favorite author on your own time. You'll begin to notice that your book discussions do not change when you read and discuss the same author on a regular basis. I'm sure most authors wouldn't agree but it's true.

Book Club Becomes Too Expensive

Book clubs can get expensive so if this is becoming a factor for your book club members quitting the book club, you may want to look at your expenses and see if it's possible to adjust your dues. If this is an individual case, try to work out a payment plan if the book club member has been loyal and is an asset to your book club.

If your member cannot afford eating out in restaurants consider discussing the book after eating your meals. Give a specific time that you will be discussing the book so that members can show up for the discussion only. Holding book club meetings in a member's home should be considered and may be a cheaper alternative to dining out.

Purchasing books can sometimes be difficult to afford. Suggest other options like obtaining book through the library system or purchasing used copies. Electronic books are also an option as well, which are always cheaper than purchasing a paper or hard cover book. Consider gifting books to members as well if it's in your book club's budget. Try to figure out other options for purchasing the book before book club members consider borrowing books from each other.

Do You Need a Reality Check?

The book club experience begins with the book club president. Everything that you implement in your book club directly affects everyone involved. It's really important that you reexamine your commitment to your book club first! Sometimes the reason why book clubs do not flourish is because of the actions or inactions (in some cases) of the president. So check yourself FIRST! Then start looking outside of yourself at other issues that may be contributing to your book club issues.

TaNisha's Pearl of Wisdom

It's really important that you keep in mind that your book club is an extension of you. What you put into your book club is exactly what you're going to get out of it. If you don't make time or allow certain issues to continue on in your book club, eventually your book club will fail. If you don't like what you see, change it!

Three Options to Take into Consideration In Order to Move Forward:

Repair the Issues Starting with You

Remember the book club experience starts with you so make sure you're on point first. When you initially created your book club you probably had a clear vision of how you wanted your book club to be. As time goes by you may or may not see those visions materialize, which can be the reason why you have a book club that you don't quite recognize anymore. You should go back and read Chapter 2 and reassess where you are, as far as, what a book club president's responsibilities are and also if your commitment to the book club has shifted. Once you've done that you should figure out what the issues are and move forward with repairing them. You should ask yourself the following questions:

- Are you just as committed to your book club as you were in the beginning?

- Are there any barriers that you're dealing with right now that is interfering with you affectively running your book club?

- Do the positives outweigh the negatives in reference to maintaining your book club?

Consider Appointing a Co-President or Vice-President

If your life dynamics have changed, it may be best to appoint a co-president or vice president to help you run the book club. This will help you to share the responsibilities of running your book club. You should make sure that this is someone that is consistent with attending meetings and have shown that they can be a leader. This should also be someone that you trust and know they can do the job.

You may want to also consider appointing officers in your book club to help share the responsibilities as well.

Dissolve the Book Club

If you really feel that being a book club president is no longer what you'd like to do, you may want to consider dissolving the book club.

Before you put a lot of thought into doing this, you should first look into possibly turning the book club over to one of your members that may be interested in keeping the book club going. It's really important that you take your members into consideration as well, especially if you have some that are really committed to the book club.

If you feel that you want to dissolve your book club because of the majority of the members i.e. inactivity, not completing book selections etc. you should definitely consider getting rid of the irresponsible book club members and keep going with the few members that remains committed. Sometimes bad members can make you want to dissolve your book club and has absolutely nothing to do with your commitment to your book club. Many book clubs have to almost start over again for various reasons. Just remember it only takes two devoted members to make a book club!

Resolve the Conflict within Your Book Club While You Still Can

Kicking out a book club member is always a hard decision to make, especially if they just happen to be a friend or family member. It's really important that you keep your book club intact and do not allow members that are a hindrance remain a part of your group, especially if their presence is causing discomfort for others or creating a negative environment.

Some of the tension can be alleviate and the bad book club member may work itself out if you're proactive and confront the issues sooner rather than later. In order to resolve the conflict with a bad book club member you should consider doing the the following steps.

Address Issues Sooner Rather Than Later!

Most situations tend to get out of hand and go on way too long because the president won't address the issues sooner rather than later. If you accept their behavior the first time by being silent, the issue will only continue on. Most people know when they are out of line but some people may not be aware. Regardless of the reason, the issue should be addressed immediately. By being silent you're giving that person permission to continue with their bad behavior.

Talk to the Member in Private

Unless the member forces you to confront them in front of others, it's really important that you address all issues away from the other members. Unless the member is being unreasonable, most issues can be resolved. Most times people may not know they are being offensive or may have a logical reason why they are behaving badly. Either way you should talk to the person about your concerns.

It's best to speak with the person in person or over the phone. Do not attempt to resolve the issue through emails or text messages. Emails and text messages can be misinterpreted, which can escalate the situation. State whatever the issue is to the member and be willing to hear them out. Be clear about what your expectations are if the person decides to remain in the book club.

Although your members may already know what's going on try to keep the conversation between your member and yourself. This will help keep the drama down and if the member decides to leave the book club (or you kick them out) it will make it easier for them to return without the other members judging them.

Create Boundaries

This is where your bylaws will come in handy. Specific bylaws will cut a lot of this ill-behavior out. Sit down with your book club member and go over the bylaw that addresses their behavior or whatever the issue may be. If you do not have the specific language written in your bylaws you should still address the issue no matter what and create boundaries with the member. You should also adopt a code of conduct clause that will deal with the issue from that point on.

Be Consistent

The reason why some bad book club members continue on the same path is because the president isn't consistent. If you set boundaries or have bylaws in place make sure you are sticking to them. This will set the tone and create a great rapport with that particular member but the entire book club.

Dismissing Members with Love

So you're pretty much at your wits end with a bad book club member and you have no other choice but to remove them from your book club! This can be especially hard if the person is a friend or a family member. For family and friends you want them out of your book club but not necessarily out of your life (or maybe you do want them out of your life but that's another story☺). There are several reasons why you may find it necessary to remove a member from your book club:

- The member doesn't read the book but want to still attend meetings.

- The member doesn't show up for meetings on a regular basis.

- The member is disrespectful, disruptive, and way too dramatic.

- The member clearly has a personality conflict or defensive towards other members.

- The member shows blatant disregard of the bylaws.

Once you've felt that you've exhausted all possibilities in order for this member to remain a part of the book club it's time to put a plan in place to kicking that member out!

Here are a few tips to help assist you with dismissing your member with love:

- Again you want to speak with the member privately.

- Let them know that you feel that it's in the best interest of the book club to no longer have them be a part of the book club and the reasons why. (This is where you would ideally be able to refer back to your bylaws.)

- Speak in a calm tone.

- If you feel that it's possible for this member to return to the book club at a later date and let them know what they will need to do in order to become a member again.

- If this is a personal friend or a family member reiterate that you love them and just because they are no longer going to be a part of the book club that you don't want there to be any tension between you two and you still want to hang out with them. (Be sure you follow through on this point)

Your new ex-member may or may not have harsh feelings. This will depend on how you approach them and if they are being defensive and unreasonable. How the person reacts is out of your hands but try not to give the person any ammunition to dispute your claims by discussing the issue while you're angry. Keep your book club in mind and do what's best for the entire book club in order to keep it intact.

Chapter 11 Exercise

DECLUTTERING YOUR BOOK CLUB

1. What are some of the barriers that your book club face that need to be addressed?

2. How to you plan on addressing these issues in order to keep your book club intact?

3. What issues have your book club have faced with bad members that can be addressed in your bylaws?

4. Write down the reasons you would find it necessary to dismiss a book club member.

CHAPTER 11 NOTES

CHAPTER 11 NOTES

BOOK CLUB AND LITERARY RESOURCES

BOOK CLUB 101 AFFILIATED WEBSITES

- **Book Club 101 University**
  www.bookclubuniversity101.net

- **Book Club 101 Magazine**
  www.bookclub101mag.com

- **The Black Book Club Experience**
  www.theblackbookclubexperience.ning.com

BOOK CLUB & READERS SOCIAL NETWORKS

- **Shelfari** www.shelfari.com

- **Goodreads** www.goodreads.com

- **Library Thing** www.literarything.com

- **ConnectViaBooks** www.connectviabooks.com

- **Book Bundlz** www.bookbundlz.com

- **weRead** www.weread.com

- **Noting:books** www.notingbooks.com

- **ReadWhale** www.readwhale.com

- **Reader2** www.reader2.com

- **aNobii** www.anobii.com

- **BookRabbit** www.bookrabbit.com

- **Revish** www.revish.com

- **BookSprouts** www.booksprouts.com

- **Readernaut** www.readernaut.com

- **Bookarmy** www.bookarmy.com

- **Booktagger** www.booktagger

- **LibroSpot** www.librospot.com

- **Bookhuddle** www.bookhuddle.com

- **Chain Reading** www.chainreading.com

- **Juicespot** www.juicespot.com

- **LivingSocial: Books** www.books.livingsocial.com

- **Booklicker** www.booklicker.com

- **BookRevyoo** www.bookrevyoo.com

- **Book Network** www.book-network.com

ONLINE BOOK CLUB FORUMS/MESSAGE BOARDS

- **Book Movement** www.bookmovement.com

- **Online Book Club** www.onlinebookclub.org

- **Online Book Club** www.arbookclub.com

- **BookTalk.org** www.booktalk.org

NOTE SECTION

I have included a note section so that you can document everything during your upcoming book club meetings, annual planning meeting, Book Club 101 University webinars, Book Club University Online Conference and the mini-courses during the KC Girlfriends Book Club Radio Show.

Please be sure to visit bookclubuniversity101.net for the schedules for all of these entities.

bookclubuniversity101.net

bookclub101mag.com

Book Club 101 University QR Code

kcgirlfriendsbookclub.com

Name:
Address:
Phone: (   )   –   cell   home   work
Email:

Name
Address
Phone: (   )   –   cell   home   work
Email

Name
Address:
Phone: (   )   –   cell   home   work
Email:

Name:
Address:
Phone: (   )   –   cell   home   work
Email:

Name:
Address:
Phone: (   )   –   cell   home   work
Email:

Name:
Address:
Phone: (   )   -   cell   home   work
Email:

- -

Name
Address
Phone: (   )   -   cell   home   work
Email

- -

Name
Address:
Phone: (   )   -   cell   home   work
Email:

- -

Name:
Address:
Phone: (   )   -   cell   home   work
Email:

- -

Name:
Address:
Phone: (   )   -   cell   home   work
Email:

Name:
Address:
Phone: (   )   –   cell   home   work
Email:

- -

Name
Address
Phone: (   )   –   cell home work
Email

- -

Name
Address:
Phone: (   )   –   cell home work
Email:

- -

Name:
Address:
Phone: (   )   –   cell home work
Email:

- -

Name:
Address:
Phone: (   )   –   cell home work
Email:

Month _____ Year _____

Meeting Location _____

Facilitator _____

Book Selection _____

Book Rating ☆ ☆ ☆ ☆ ☆

We would read this author again? Yes No Maybe

- -

Notes

_____
_____
_____
_____
_____
_____
_____
_____
_____
_____
_____
_____
_____
_____
_____
_____
_____
_____
_____
_____
_____
_____

Month _____ Year _____

Meeting Location _____

Facilitator _____

Book Selection _____

Book Rating ☆ ☆ ☆ ☆ ☆

We would read this author again? Yes No Maybe

Notes

_____
_____
_____
_____
_____
_____
_____
_____
_____
_____
_____
_____
_____
_____
_____
_____
_____
_____
_____
_____
_____

Month _____ Year _____

Meeting Location _____

Facilitator _____

Book Selection _____

Book Rating ☆ ☆ ☆ ☆ ☆

We would read this author again? Yes No Maybe

- -

Notes

_____
_____
_____
_____
_____
_____
_____
_____
_____
_____
_____
_____
_____
_____
_____
_____
_____
_____
_____
_____
_____

Month _____ Year _____

Meeting Location _____

Facilitator _____

Book Selection _____

Book Rating ☆ ☆ ☆ ☆ ☆

We would read this author again? Yes No Maybe

Notes

_____
_____
_____
_____
_____
_____
_____
_____
_____
_____
_____
_____
_____
_____
_____
_____
_____
_____
_____

Month_____ Year_____

Meeting Location_____

Facilitator_____

Book Selection_____

Book Rating ☆ ☆ ☆ ☆ ☆

We would read this author again? Yes No Maybe

- -

Notes

_____

_____

_____

_____

_____

_____

_____

_____

_____

_____

_____

_____

_____

_____

_____

_____

_____

_____

_____

_____

Month _____ Year _____

Meeting Location _____

Facilitator _____

Book Selection _____

Book Rating ☆ ☆ ☆ ☆ ☆

We would read this author again? Yes No Maybe

Notes

_____
_____
_____
_____
_____
_____
_____
_____
_____
_____
_____
_____
_____
_____
_____
_____
_____
_____
_____
_____
_____
_____

Month _____ Year _____

Meeting Location _____

Facilitator _____

Book Selection _____

Book Rating ☆ ☆ ☆ ☆ ☆

We would read this author again? Yes No Maybe

Notes

_____
_____
_____
_____
_____
_____
_____
_____
_____
_____
_____
_____
_____
_____
_____
_____
_____
_____
_____
_____
_____

Month _____ Year _____

Meeting Location _____

Facilitator _____

Book Selection _____

Book Rating ☆ ☆ ☆ ☆ ☆

We would read this author again? Yes No Maybe

- -

Notes

_____

_____

_____

_____

_____

_____

_____

_____

_____

_____

_____

_____

_____

_____

_____

_____

_____

_____

_____

_____

_____

_____

Month _____ Year _____

Meeting Location _____

Facilitator _____

Book Selection _____

Book Rating ☆ ☆ ☆ ☆ ☆

We would read this author again? Yes No Maybe

Notes

_____
_____
_____
_____
_____
_____
_____
_____
_____
_____
_____
_____
_____
_____
_____
_____
_____
_____
_____
_____
_____

Month _____ Year _____

Meeting Location _____

Facilitator _____

Book Selection _____

Book Rating ☆ ☆ ☆ ☆ ☆

We would read this author again? Yes No Maybe

Notes

_____
_____
_____
_____
_____
_____
_____
_____
_____
_____
_____
_____
_____
_____
_____
_____
_____
_____
_____
_____
_____

Month _____ Year _____

Meeting Location _____

Facilitator _____

Book Selection _____

Book Rating ☆ ☆ ☆ ☆ ☆

We would read this author again? Yes No Maybe

- -

Notes

_____

_____

_____

_____

_____

_____

_____

_____

_____

_____

_____

_____

_____

_____

_____

_____

_____

_____

_____

_____

_____

Month _____ Year _____

Meeting Location _____

Facilitator _____

Book Selection _____

Book Rating ☆ ☆ ☆ ☆ ☆

We would read this author again? Yes No Maybe

Notes

_____
_____
_____
_____
_____
_____
_____
_____
_____
_____
_____
_____
_____
_____
_____
_____
_____
_____
_____

Budget

Income	Income Amounts		
Dues			
Fundraiser			
Donations			
Misc			
Misc			
Misc			
Misc			
Expenses		**Expense Amounts**	
Sponsored Events			
Community Service			
Author Expenses			
Member Travel Expenses (pd by group)			
Website Expenses			
Misc			
Misc			
Misc			
Misc			
Income & Expense Totals			

Place your bank balance, income and expense totals below to figure out your total income or loss for the upcoming year.

Bank Balance +	+
Income Total +	+
Expense Total -	-
Total Income or Debt	+/-

Changes & Plans

Document any changes for the next year:

Budget   ⭘ No Changes Required ⭘ Changes Required

_____

_____

_____

_____

Mission Statement ⭕ No Changes Required ⭕ Changes Required

_____

_____

_____

New Membership ⭕ No Changes Required ⭕ Changes Required

_____

_____

_____

Book Club Meetings ⭕ No Changes Required ⭕ Changes Required

_____

_____

_____

Community Service ⭕ No Changes Required ⭕ Changes Required

_____

_____

_____

Events ⭕ No Changes Required ⭕ Changes Required

_____

_____

_____

Review of Bylaws ⭕ No Changes Required ⭕ Changes Required

_____

_____

_____

Miscellaneous ⭕ No Changes Required ⭕ Changes Required

_____

_____

_____

Annual Planning Meeting Notes, Follow Up Discussions/ Decisions

Topic _____

Objectives

○ _____
○ _____
○ _____
○ _____
○ _____

Notes _____

_____

_____

_____

_____

_____

_____

_____

Topic _____

Objectives

○ _____
○ _____
○ _____
○ _____
○ _____

Notes _____

_____

_____

_____

_____

_____

_____

Topic _____

Objectives

○ _____
○ _____
○ _____
○ _____
○ _____

Notes _____

_____
_____
_____
_____
_____
_____
_____
_____

Topic _____

Objectives

○ _____
○ _____
○ _____
○ _____
○ _____

Notes _____

_____
_____
_____
_____
_____
_____
_____

Topic _____

Objectives

○ _____
○ _____
○ _____
○ _____
○ _____

Notes _____

_____
_____
_____
_____
_____
_____
_____

Topic _____

Objectives

○ _____
○ _____
○ _____
○ _____
○ _____

Notes _____

_____
_____
_____
_____
_____
_____
_____

Notes

Notes

Notes

Notes

ABOUT THE AUTHOR

TaNisha Webb is the founder of Book Club 101 University and the Publisher and Editor in Chief of Book Club 101 Magazine. She is also the founder and host of Book Club University Online Conference.

TaNisha is the president of the KC Girlfriends Book Club and is currently the moderator of the Maximizing Your Book Club Experience panel discussion for the National Book Club Conference in Atlanta, GA.

TaNisha currently lives in Kansas City, MO.

Please feel free to contact TaNisha
Websites: www.tanishawebbonline.com
www.bookclubuniversity101.net
Facebook: tanisha.webb Twitter @twebbonline